THE SHOTOKAN KARATE HANDBOOK:
BEGINNER TO BLACK BELT

GICHIN FUNAKOSHI

Father of modern-day Karate

1868-1957

Pictured above is Gichin Funakoshi, the father of modern-day Karate. In addition to Karate, he was deeply involved in calligraphy and the writing of poetry. He would sign his work by using his pen name, Shoto. It is from that pen name that the creation of the word "Shotokan" arose. The name is made up using the word Shoto, meaning waving pines (his verse was often inspired by the gently waving pines on the hills near his home), and the word Kan, meaning house or school. His first school of Karate, based at his home, therefore became known as Shoto's Kan, which was eventually shortened to Shotokan.

In 1955, the Japan Karate Association was established with Funakoshi as Chief Instructor.

The handful of students and instructors who trained under him then passed their experience and knowledge on to the continuing stream of hungry, prospective Karate-Kas. Funakoshi, remembered as the master of Karate, died in 1957 at the age of 88.

THE SHOTOKAN KARATE HANDBOOK:
BEGINNER TO BLACK BELT

BY
GURSHARAN SAHOTA
8TH DAN

CHIEF INSTRUCTOR
TRADITIONAL INTERNATIONAL SHOTOKAN KARATE
ASSOCIATION

Published By
GURSHARAN SAHOTA
www.Tiska.com

First Published October 1994
Second Edition 1996
Third Edition 2000
Fourth Edition 2003
Fifth Edition 2005
Sixth Edition 2008
Seventh Edition February 2009
Eighth Edition May 2015

By the Same Author
The Advanced Shotokan Karate Handbook

ACKNOWLEDGEMENTS

The author wishes to thank the following:
The association Black Belts namely; Pedro Barker, Kevin Coles, Carole Barker, John Garne, Martin Palfrey, Colin Thorp, Kym Watson, Paul Leon, Simon Russell, Kevin Anderson, Paul Debock, Samantha Lavender, Jacqui Malam, Derek Brogie, Martin Toyer, Alison Csom, Amrik Singh, Lorraine Tomic, Abul Ghomshei, Demetrius Palikaru, Kirk Cosford, Nigel Howlett, Alan Jones, Phil Shaw, Donna Debock, John Bailey, Kym Lowde, John Owen, Graham Tait, Peter Ireson, Jed Otham, Mark Thompson, Lynne Buckledee, Kevin Burton, Keith Tunstall, Sudager Bharj, Harish Popat, Mehardip Matharu, Robert Chalmers, Clive Hamp, Alvan Hartley, Martin McKay, Jillian Thorp, Michael Crighton, Marilyn Redman, Darren Wildman, Paul David, Adetunji Omole, Elizabeth Joannides, Mark Joannides, Michael Cook, Anne Meagher, Eddie Kerr and Lee Stockley for their involvement in the creation of this book.

Roy Hazelwood, Chief Instructor of Traditional Shotokan Karate Association GB, and Lawrence Elcock for their enthusiasm and support.
His family, especially his two elder brothers, Avtar and Bhupinder, Taekwon-Do 8th Dan Chief Instructor of Global (ITF) Institutes, who with their drive and determination got him started on the road to Karate.
Paul Hooley, of Paul Hooley Associates, for his technical advice. Alan Cooke, of A C Photography, for his time and co-operation during the lengthy photo sessions (and now, knowing all the moves, he looks forward to seeing you at the next beginners' intake)!
Mick Billman, for writing the foreword, and Colin Malam, of the Sunday Telegraph, for reading the proofs.
Finally, Lorraine Tomic for her help in the preparation of the photographs and editorial.

ISBN 0 9524638 0 6

Published by Gursharan Sahota, email : tiska.karate@btconnect.com
www.tiska.com

U.K. Distributor:
Gazelle Book Services Limited, Falcon House, Queen Square, Lancaster LA1 1RN, England.
Telephone No: 01524-68765   Fax No: 01524-63232

Produced by Paul Hooley and Sahota Publishing, England
Printed in China

I dedicate this book to my parents, PIARA and AMAR.

PREFACE

GURSHARAN SAHOTA 8ᵗʰ DAN

At last Karate is recognised as a sport, constantly rising in popularity. With this in mind I have written this book to provide the ultimate companion for the Karate-Ka, (person) based on step-by-step techniques to assist from the beginner to Black Belt level.

This book also aims to make the Karate-Ka aware that time, effort and practice are the main factors in working towards perfecting not only one's skills, but also one's inner mind and attitude towards such an Art.

GURSHARAN SAHOTA
October 1994

FOREWORD

MICK BILLMAN – 8th DAN

There have been numerous books written on the subject of Karate, including many that claim to show an easy, step-by-step, way of becoming a black belt by the third chapter!

It would be stating the obvious to say that, to become proficient in the "Way of the Empty Hand", one must persevere over a long period of time, through many hours of physical conditioning, as well as learning to develop the mind to cope with "Highs" and "Lows" experienced as a result of continuous, strenuous activity.

In a martial art such as Karate, it is extremely rare to find a book that can help the student with the physical aspect of Karate to any great degree. However, every now and then a publication appears on the bookstands that can do just that. One such book is the Shotokan Karate Handbook (Beginner to Black Belt).

I have known the author, Gursharan Sahota, for over 24 years and during that time he has never veered from the strict traditions of Shotokan Karate.

The following pages contain a wealth of information on the Kihon, Kata, and Kumite aspects of Traditional Shotokan. Written in an easy to follow manner, and supplemented by an extremely comprehensive set of photographs, this handbook is easily one of the more superior publications available.

Karate can be many things to many people. For some it is the ideal way to achieve complete physical fitness, while to others it provides the key to unlocking the door to self-discipline and self-realisation.

Whichever direction you choose, this handbook will certainly prove to be a most valuable asset on your journey along "The Way"

MICK BILLMAN, 8TH DAN
October 1994

*Mick Billman is a 8th Dan Black Belt in Shotokan Karate and is at
the time of publication a member of the Executive Committee of
the English Karate Governing Body.*

THE HISTORY OF KARATE

The two Chinese characters **KARA** and **TE** make up the ideographs in Japan for the word Karate, and thus denote that it is of Chinese origin. It appears that this evidence points towards the fact that Karate was practised in China first before it was ever practised in Japan or the Ryukyu Islands.

It is known that, in the Sixth Century, an Indian Buddhist Monk, Bodhidharma, journeyed from Asia to China. His role was to establish the Zen School of Buddhism. Bodhidharma travelled to the Shaolin Temple, where his teaching began. Many of the monks were very weak and found such physical exercise too exhausting. Bodhidharma devised a training method that would assist the monks both physically and mentally so that they could continue their Zen practice.

The word Karate means "empty hand" – Kara meaning empty and Te meaning hand. It is an art which teaches its students self defence by using their arms and legs as controlled weapons.

The master behind Karate was Gichin Funakoshi. He was born in Shuri, Okinawa Prefecture in 1868. It was whilst he was lecturing at the Okinawa Teachers' College that he was given the opportunity, in 1922, to lecture and demonstrate his art of Karate. The event was sponsored by the Ministry of Education. After such a demonstration, Funakoshi received a multitude of requests for him to teach in Tokyo.

In 1936 Funakoshi formed "Shotokan", a true landmark in Karate's history.

Gursharan Sahota demonstrating Ushiro Mawashi Geri

*"Do not think that you have to win,
rather think that you do not have to lose"*

CONTENTS

CONTENTS

THE KUMITE TEAM

Gursharan Sahota (Team Captain), Roy Hazelwood, Donovan Slue, Robin Reid, & Lawrence Ellcock

KUMITE TEAM 20 YEARS ON.

WARM UP EXERCISES

It is imperative that you warm and stretch your body before you take part in any form of physical exercise.

Karate training exercises should be performed before and at the end of each training session and can of course be practised on their own.

A Karate-Ka should be made aware of the importance of such exercises which are designed to "warm up" the body, stretch the muscles, tendons and ligaments, and control blood flow and heart rate.

The performance of the exercises should be carried out gently and slowly to help avoid injuries.

Gentle stretching at the end of a training session enables the body to relax and wind down.

Exercises are always carried out in a systematic way, beginning with the more mobile areas of the body such as the head and neck and working downwards.

1. Lift the knees repeatedly.

2.

3. Bounce on spot.

4.

WARM UP EXERCISES

5. Perform 'Jumping Jacks'.

6.

7. Move legs alternately backwards and forwards.

8.

9. Bounce backwards and forwards in free style stance.

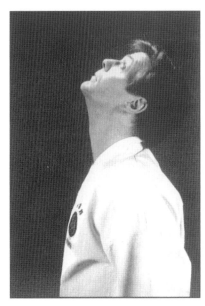

10. Stretch neck backwards and forwards slowly.

11.

12. Move head slowly side to side.

13.

14. Move head shoulder to shoulder.

15.

WARM UP EXERCISES

16. Half neck roll.

17.

18.

19. Lift shoulders up and down keeping head still.

20. Relax shoulders down.

21. Bend the wrist and push palm downwards.

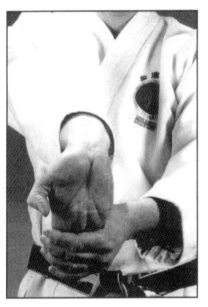

22. Push back of hand towards forearm.

23. Stretch the back of the arm. Repeat on other side.

24. Stretch the shoulders. Repeat on both sides.

25. Cross arms in front of chest and swing them behind. This stretches the upper arms and chest.

26.

27.

WARM UP EXERCISES

28. Swing arms overhead.

29.

30.

31.

32.

33. Lean to the side using the hand for support and bend directly over the other leg.

34.

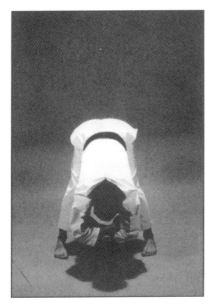

35. Bend over from waist and keep knees relaxed.

36. Support bottom of back with both hands, lean back and push hips forward.

37. Rotate upper body.

38.

39

WARM UP EXERCISES

40.

41.

42. In forward stance rotate hip in and out using hand for guidance. Repeat on other side.

43.

44.

45. Raise heel of back foot and push lower into stance by leaning forward. Repeat on other side.

46. Push down on instep of back foot to lower stance. The back knee should not touch the floor. Repeat on other side.

47. Head to knee.

48.

49. In Kiba-dachi, push out knees with elbows and lower hips.

50. Perform the same exercise as before in Shiko-dachi stance (feet turned outwards).

51. Place hands on the floor for support.

WARM UP EXERCISES

52. Hands can be lifted off the floor as flexibility and strength develops.

53. Straddle position. Repeat on other side.

54. Use elbow to push knee out and stretch inner thigh.

55. Bend from the waist putting chest towards thigh.

56. Place back heel on floor and stretch back.

57. Stretch toes. Repeat on other side.

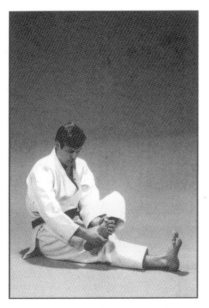

58. Rotate ankle. Repeat on other side.

59. Hurdle stretch. Repeat on other side.

60.

61. Bend to side. Repeat on other side.

62. Place head towards knee and stretch. Repeat on other side.

63. Bend forward. Repeat on other side.

64. Stretch the spine and repeat on other side.

65. Take front foot behind and lower head. Repeat on other side.

66. Place both hands on the floor and push down. Repeat the sequence on other side.

67. Lean back and point front foot upwards. Lower head towards knee. Repeat on other side.

68. In front splits support your body with your hands. Repeat on other side.

69. Sit on the floor with legs as far apart as possible. Place head towards your knee. Repeat on other side.

70. Place hands in front and lower chest to floor.

71. Bring both feet towards the groin and push knees down using elbows.

72. Lower head towards feet.

73. Point toes and bend forwards.

74. Flex toes and bend forwards.

75. Sit on insteps.

76. Lean back and support upper body with elbows.

77. Sit on the balls of your feet.

78. Lean back and support your body with your hands.

79. Lift knee to the front and pull towards chest. Repeat on other side.

80. Pull knee to side and raise foot into Mawashi-geri position. Repeat on other side.

81.

82. In forward stance perform front leg raising. Repeat on other side.

83.

84. Note position for raising leg to the side.

85. Perform side leg raising and make sure foot is in Sokuto position. Repeat on other side.

86. Note position for rear leg raising.

87. Perform rear leg raising and make sure back is arched. Repeat on other side.
The warm up is now complete.

WARM UP EXERCISES

Remember it is important to wind down at the end of every training session with gentle stretching exercises.

KIHON
Basic Techniques

All basic techniques consist of punching, striking, blocking and kicking (remembering at all times that both the hands and feet are potentially lethal weapons.

All Kihon techniques can be performed in the stepping or stationary positions. Correct stances and posture should be maintained whilst applying such techniques. Last, but certainly not least, correct breathing should be maintained during these techniques.

Throughout this handbook, all the Kihon (basics), Kumite (sparring) and Kata (formal exercises) are shown in an easy, step-by-step manner, working upwards from beginner to black belt level.

DACHI : *Stances*

The following, with the use of photographs, outlines the Stances used in the art of Karate. All Karate-Ka must remember that a great deal of time should be devoted to enable the development of good strong stances.

The Stances, one should bear in mind, are the root of all Karate techniques

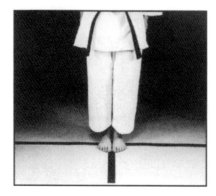

1a. Heisoku Dachi
(informal attention stance)

1b. Musubi Dachi
(informal attention stance, feet turned out)

2. Hachiji Dachi
(open leg stance)

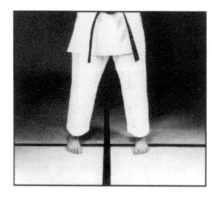

3. Heiko Dachi
(parallel stance)

4. Uchi Hachiji Dachi
(inverted open leg stance)

5. Zenkutsu Dachi
(front/forward stance)

6. Kokutsu Dachi
(back stance)

7. Kiba Dachi
(straddle leg stance, also known as horse riding stance)

8. Shiko Dachi
   (square stance)

9. Fudo Dachi
   (rooted stance)
   (Sometimes known as Sochin Dachi
   – diagonal straddle leg stance)

10. Teiji Dachi
    (T stance)

11. Renoji Dachi
    (L stance)

12. Kosa Dachi
    (crossed feet stance)

13. Sanchin Dachi
    (hour glass stance)

14. Hangetsu Dachi
    (half moon stance) (also known
    as wide hour glass stance)

15. Neko Ashi Dachi
    (cat's foot stance)

16. Tsuru Ashi Dachi
    (crane leg stance)
    (As in Kata, Gankaku)

ZUKI : *Punching*

In all cases punches are delivered from A to B at speed and following the shortest route possible. The majority of Karate punches learnt as a beginner are executed in a straight line.

The positioning of the fist is a very important factor to remember.

FORMING A FIST

1. Open hand

Application

2. Curl fingers

3. Curl fingers into palm of hand

4. Tighten finger tips into palm of hand

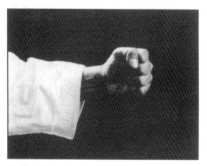

5. Put thumb on top of curled fingers and tense wrist

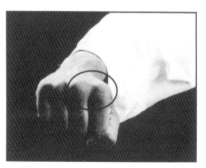

6. **FIST.** This is the part of the fist which is used whilst punching with the first two knuckles

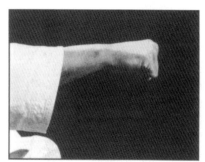

7. Fist position whilst punching

CHOKU ZUKI
Straight Punch

This is the first punch a beginner would learn in the stance Hachiji Dachi. The punching hand starts from the waist level (fig 1); the arm then travels in a straight line, aiming at all times at the target. At the same time, the opposite arm pulls back in the reverse direction (fig 2). The wrist rotates at 180° at the end of the technique with one's breath exhaled and body tensed (fig 3).

1. Choku Zuki in Hachiji Dachi position

2. ²/₃rd position

3. Choku Zuki

Application

GYAKU ZUKI
Reverse Punch

This is possibly the strongest punch in Karate. This technique is performed from Zenkutsu Dachi. Once in the stance, the left hand is extended in an open position (Tate Shuto Uke, vertical knife hand block) ready for the punch (fig 1), your hips being at 45°. Begin to execute the right hand punch, keeping the same hip position

(fig 2) without moving the front knee. Concentrate the eyes on the target at all times. With a strong thrust from the back leg, fully extend the arm, twist the right hip, breathe out, tense the body and rotate the fist 180°, thus completing the punch.

1. Zenkutsu Dachi – left hand out

2. ²/₃rd position

3. Gyaku Zuki

Application

OI ZUKI
Lunge Punch

Oi Zuki is performed in the same manner as Choku Zuki, the difference being that Oi Zuki is performed in a stepping motion.

Beginning from the Gedan Barai position (fig. 1), bring the back leg forward (fig. 2) keeping the same height with hips square on. Step through with the right leg, thrusting the hips forward and landing in the opposite stance while executing the Oi Zuki punch. Remember to exhale your breath and tense the body (fig. 3).

1. Gedan Barai

2. Half way position

3. Oi Zuki

Application

AGE ZUKI
Rising Punch

Age Zuki is a rising punch moving in an upward arc usually to make contact with the opponents chin.

1. Gedan Barai

2. Age Zuki

Application

TATE ZUKI
Vertical Fist Punch

Tate Zuki is a straight punch with the fist rotating through 90° Ideally used for close range attacks.

1.Gedan Barai

2. Tate Zuki

Application

URA ZUKI
Close/Uppercut Punch

A technique most effective for close range attacks where the fist is not rotated but executed in a straight line to the target.

1. Gedan Barai

2. Ura Zuki

Application

MAWASHI ZUKI
Roundhouse Punch

This is a circular rising punch and this makes contact with the side of the opponents head.

1. Gedan Barai

2. Mawashi Zuki

Application

KAGE ZUKI
Hook Punch

Kage Zuki is used to attack the solar plexus, ribs and face at close range from Kiba Dachi (horse riding stance).

1. Kiba Dachi

2. Kage Zuki

Application

MOROTE ZUKI
Double Punch

From Zenkutsu Dachi stance, with inverted fists placed on both hips, the arms simultaneously attack the target (stomach region) whilst stepping forward

1. Right forward stance

2. Right forward stance
   Morote Zuki

YAMA ZUKI
Wide U Punch

Yama Zuki is executed by attacking both the head and the stomach area simultaneously. To effect this move, the body must be slightly inclined.

1. Left forward stance
   fist to right side

2. Yama Zuki

Application

Application

KIZAMI ZUKI
Jabbing Punch

Usually performed from freestyle stance (Jiyu Dachi). Attack by pushing forward from Jiyu Dachi, jabbing with the right fist and pulling back your left fist. This is a short fast punch.

1. Right freestyle Stance

2. Kizami Zuki

Sightseeing in Japan

Application

UKE : *Blocking*

As a Karate-Ka all blocking techniques should be used as a form of defence as opposed to being offensive. In the main, most attacks are deflected away from the target, creating an opening for your counter attack. The following chapter outlines blocking techniques with your arms and feet used as the defensive weapons.

GEDAN BARAI UKE
Lower Level/Downward Block

From the Yoi (ready) position, raise your left arm with the fist in the outward facing position level with your right ear. Step forward with left leg and, blocking in a fast forward motion, step into front stance. The blocking fist should finish in a position approximately 4 inches above the knee. Pulling the opposite hand back to the waist, ensure that the hip is in hanmi position, (half front facing).

1. YOI

2. Left arm up

3. Gedan Barai Uke

Application

AGE UKE
Upper Rising Block

Age Uke is used in deflecting an attack to the facial area. From Gedan Barai step forward and raise the right arm with the hips square on. Pull the right arm back and block, with the left arm rising in front of the head and finishing approximately three to four inches above your forehead.

Pulling the opposite hand back to the waist, ensure that the hip is in hanmi position, half front facing.

1. Right Gedan Barai

2. ²/₃ position left arm up
   – hips square on

3. Age Uke

Application

SOTO UDE UKE
Outside Forearm Block

Raise the blocking arm, with the fist almost level with your ear, the right hand open at chudan level and the hips side on. Stepping into forward stance, bring the blocking arm in an arc to a position approximately eighteen inches in front of the centre line of the body. Pulling the opposite hand back to the waist, ensure that the hip is in hanmi position, half front facing.

1. Gedan Barai   2. ²/₃ position

3. Soto Ude Uke

Application

UCHI UDE UKE
Inside Forearm Block

Step forward with the blocking arm just above the hip, the left hand open chudan level and the hips square on. Complete the technique by bringing the blocking arm across the body in an arc, finishing with the block level with the side of the body.
Pulling the opposite hand back to the waist, ensure that the hip is in hanmi position, half front facing.

1. Left Gedan Barai   2. Half way position

3. Uchi Ude Uke

Application

SHUTO UKE
Knife Hand Block

From Gedan Barai step to the half-way position, hips square on. The opposite hand is thrust forward, palm down, and the blocking hand, palm inward, is placed beside the opposite ear. The right foot should step into back stance and the blocking arm be rotated forward, using the elbow as a pivot whilst keeping the palm facing forwards. Pull the opposite hand back to the upper stomach area, palm upwards.

1. Left Gedan Barai

2. Feet together – halfway position

3. Shuto Uke

Application

OTHER BLOCKING TECHNIQUES

The following are a number of other blocking techniques used in the art of Karate.

1. Kakiwake Uke – *Wedge block*

2. Jodan Juji Uke – *Upper level X block*

3. Jodan Kaisho Juji Uke – *Open hand X block*

4. Gedan Juji Uke – *Lower level X block*

5. Tate Shuto Uke – *Vertical knife hand block*

6. Morote Uke – *Augmented two handed block*

7. Otoshi Uke – *Dropping block*

8. Teisho Awase Uke – *Combined palm heel block*

9. Sukui Uke – *Scooping block with fist*

10. Sukui Uke – *Scooping block with open hand*

11. Gedan Kake Uke – *Downward hooking block*

12. Te Osae Uke – *Hand pressing block*

OTHER BLOCKING TECHNIQUES

13. Mika Zuki Geri Uke – *Crescent kick block*

14. Kakuto Uke – *Bent wrist block)*

15. Sokumen Awase Uke – *Side combined block*

16. Te Nagashi Uke – *Hand sweeping block*

17. Ashibo Kake Uke – *Leg hooking block*

18. Haiwan Nagashi Uke – *Back arm sweeping block*

19. Sokutei Osae Uke – *Pressing block with sole*

20. Sokuto Osae Uke – *Pressing block with footedge*

21. Ashikubi Kake Uke – *Ankle hooking block*

GERI : *Kicking*

Kicks require a great deal of practice in both balance and timing to perfect their performance. Shifting one's body weight or balancing on one leg can often cause difficulties to a Karate-Ka, hence the need for repetitive training.

Once these are controlled, a kick can be one of the most effective and powerful blocks or attacks. When executing a kick, one should always remember to withdraw the kicking leg immediately to avoid your opponent's grasp/sweep and keep your balance.

MAE GERI
Front Kick

Most commonly used from front stance, but can be used effectively from various stances.

From forward stance, with arms by your side, bring the kicking leg forward in an upward movement. As the knee passes the belt level, extend the lower part of the leg, striking the target with the ball of the foot. This technique can be used effectively as a thrust (Mae Geri Kekomi) or snap (Mae Geri Keage) kick, given the individual circumstances.

1. Right stance

2. Left knee up

3. Left kick – Mae Geri

Application

YOKO GERI KEAGE
Side Snap Kick

In training, this kick is more frequently practised in Kiba Dachi (fig. 1). The left foot crosses in front of the opposite foot (Sash Ashi) (fig. 2), the kicking knee then comes up and points to the target (fig. 3). The leg is snapped out in an upward arc, and then back (Fig.4). Contact is made using the edge of the foot (Sokuto).

1. Left Kiba Dachi

2. Cross over (Sashi Ashi)

3. Knee points to the target

4. Yoko Geri Keage

Application

YOKO GERI KEKOMI
Side Thrust Kick

As with Yoko Geri Keage this kick is normally practised in the stance Kiba Dachi. The left foot crosses in front of the opposite foot (fig. 1). Keeping the hips at the same height, raise your knee (fig. 2), thrust the hip in and strike the target (fig. 3) at the same time pivoting on the opposite foot. Contact, as with Yoko Geri Keage, is made with Sokuto. When performed correctly, this is one of the most powerful kicks.

1. Cross over

2. Raise Knee

3. Yoko Geri Kekomi

Application

MAWASHI GERI
Roundhouse Kick

Mawashi Geri is performed from Zenkutsu Dachi (fig. 1). Lift the kicking knee up to the side (fig. 2), ensuring your posture is upright. Keeping the kicking knee to the side, pivot on the supporting leg (ball of the foot) and revolve your body and hips. Snap your leg to the target (fig. 3), contacting with the ball of the foot.

1. Zenkutsu Dachi

2. Knee up

3. Mawashi Geri

Application

USHIRO GERI
Back Kick

The heel is used as the contact point in Ushiro Geri, this kick being one of the strongest. This is due to the fact that both hips are being thrust backwards. From Zenkutsu Dachi (fig 1.), pivot on the front foot and lift the kicking leg (fig 2) with the hips facing backwards. Thrust the leg towards the target (fig 3), with both hips being thrust backwards at the same time.

1. Left Zenkutsu Dachi

2. Lift kicking leg

3. Ushiro Geri

Application

USHIRO MAWASHI GERI
Reverse Roundhouse Kick

The heel is used as the striking area in this technique. From Zenkutsu Dachi (fig 1) draw the kicking leg up and behind you (fig 2) revolving the body around and making contact with the target (fig 3). In competition, this technique should be performed with the sole of the foot as opposed to the heel.

1. Zenkutsu Dachi

2. Leg up and behind

3. Ushiro Mawashi Geri

Application

Mikazuki Geri *Crescent kick*

Featured here are various additional kicks with their Japanese terminology.

Gyaku Mawashi Geri *Reverse Roundhouse kick*

Mikazuki Geri Uke *Crescent kick block*

Hiza Geri *Knee kick*

Ashi Barai *Sweeping leg kick*

Mawashi Hiza Geri *Roundhouse knee kick*

OTHER KICKING TECHNIQUES

Featured here are various additional kicks with their Japanese terminology.

(Right) Mae Tobi Geri
Front jumping kick

(Far Right) Yoko Tobi Geri
Side jumping kick

(Below) Ushiro Kekomi Geri
Back side thrust kick

(Above) Kakato Geri *Heel kick*

(Left) Mae Geri Kekomi *Front thrust kick*

UCHI : *Striking*

Striking techniques are executed as counter attacks in the art of self defence.
In competition they are used in attacks to score points on an opponent.

A high percentage of the power and speed of the technique is gained by the swift withdrawal of the non-striking arm

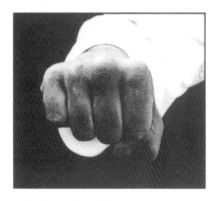

1. Seiken – *Forefist*

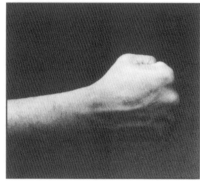

2. Uraken – *Backfist*

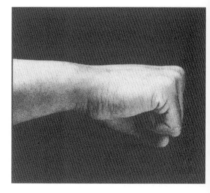

3. Tettsui – *Bottom Fist*
   (a) Kentsui – *Hammer fist*

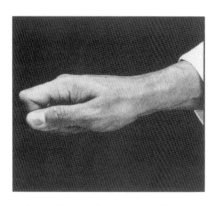

4. Ippon Ken – *One knuckle fist*

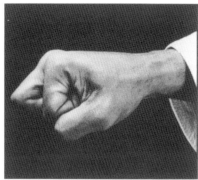

5. Nakadaka Ippon Ken – *Middle finger one knuckle fist*

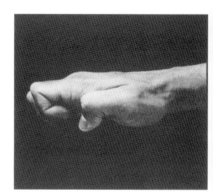

6. Hiraken – *Fore knuckle fist*

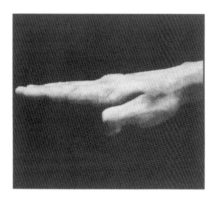

7. Haito – *Ridge hand*

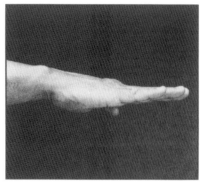

8. Shuto – *Knifehand*

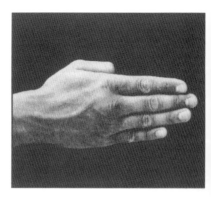

9. Haishu – *Back hand*

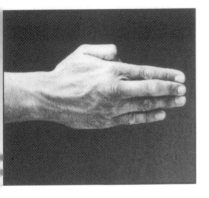

10. Nukite – *Spear hand*

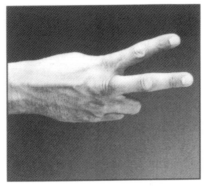

11. Nihon Nukite – *Two finger spear hand*

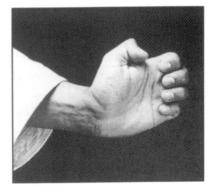

12. Teisho – *Palm heel*

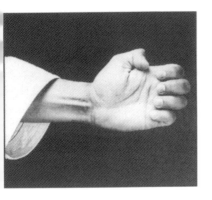

13. Kumade – *Bear hand*

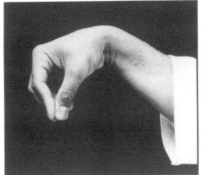

14. Kakuto – *Bent wrist*

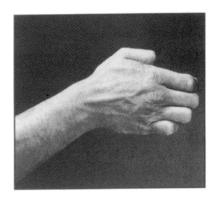

15. Keito – *Chicken head wrist*

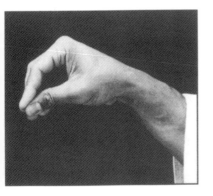

16. Washide – *Eagle beak*

17. Seiryuto – *Ox jaw hand*

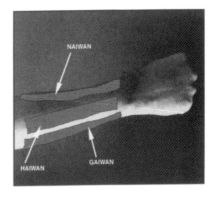

18. Gaiwan – *outside forearm*
Naiwan – *inside forearm*
Haiwan – *upper forearm*

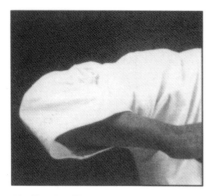

19. Empi – *Elbow*

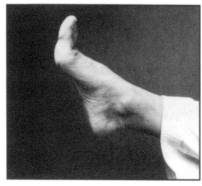

20. Koshi – *Ball of the foot*

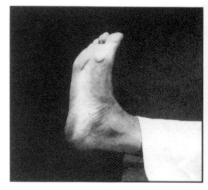

21. Sokutei – *Sole of the foot*

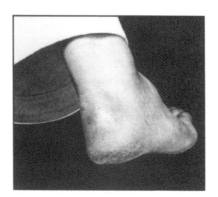

22. Kakato – *Heel*

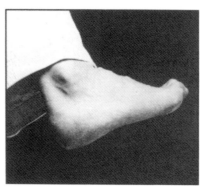

23. Sokuto – *Edge of the foot*

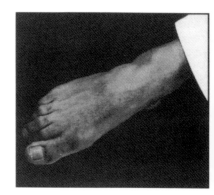

24. Heisoku – *Instep*

25. Hiza – *Knee*

Empi is used in a variety of ways to attack the chin, chest, ribs and solar plexus. Examples as set out below:–

EMPI UCHI : *Elbow Strike*

1. Age Empi Uchi – *Upper rising elbow strike, also known as Tate Empi Uchi*

2. Yoko Empi Uchi – *Side elbow strike*

3. Otoshi Empi Uchi – *Downward (dropping) elbow strike*

4. Ushiro Empi Uchi – *Backward elbow strike*

5. Mawashi Empi Uchi – *Roundhouse elbow strike*

HAND STRIKING TECHNIQUES

1. Uraken Uchi – *Backfist strike (front)*

2. Uraken Uchi – *Backfist strike (side)*

3. Tettsui Uchi – *Bottom fist strike*

4. Haito Uchi – *Ridge hand strike*

5. Haishu Uchi – *Back hand strike*

6. Shuto Uchi – *Knife hand strike (outside)*

HAND STRIKING TECHNIQUES

7. Shuto Uchi – *Knife hand strike (inside)*

8. Awase Zuki – *U Punch*

9. Teisho Uchi – *Palm heel strike*

10. Hasami Zuki – *Scissors punch*

SELF DEFENCE

Self defence is itself a continuation of Karate. Knowing the basic skills enables a student, if ever required, to help deal with difficult situations. The world today is not the safest of places for any of us, whether we be young or old, man or woman.

As with Karate, self defence needs to be practised hard and often for it to have the right effect. A student should feel as confident as possible with their situation. The only way to ensure that defence works for you, is to practice with a partner.

Remember, we are not all built the same and weights and ages must be considered. Consequently what works for one, will not necessarily work for us all.

Make sure you are familiar with <u>all</u> the techniques. You never know when you might need any one of them.

Likewise be prepared – being panic stricken is often the key delay factor when being attacked.

The more you practice, the better you will get. This will teach you to apply the right technique with confidence to catch your attacker off guard.

Trust your own judgement and be your own critic – you will soon know how you can perform best, but most importantly always practice hard!

SEQUENCE 1

1.1 Defence against strangle hold

1.2 Arm over

1.3 Swing across at angle using your body weight

SEQUENCE 2

1.4 Strike Empi (Elbow)

2.1 Defence against strangle hold

2.2 Raise arm over

Section 1 : Basic Techniques – Self Defence   **31**

SELF DEFENCE

2.3 Block Soto Uke over arms, thus putting pressure on attackers wrists

2.4 Spinning body round

2.5 Striking Empi Jodan

SEQUENCE 3

2.6 Raising right arm up

2.7 Strike to groin

3.1 Strangle hold

3.2 Thread right hand through attackers arms

3.3 Place palms together

3.4 Take head back

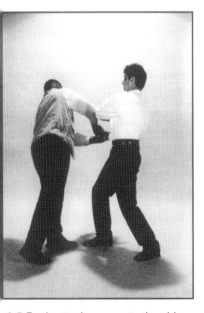

3.5 Push attackers arm to the side, thus releasing strangle hold

3.6 Strike with hand

3.7 Pull attacker down with Hiza Geri (knee)

SEQUENCE 4

4.1 Attacker grabbing wrist with both hands

4.2 Form fist with right hand, bring left hand inside their arms, and grab fist

4.3 Pulling towards body

SEQUENCE 5

4.4 Strike Empi (elbow)

5.1 Attacker grabbing wrist with both hands

5.2 Open right hand and rotate outwards

SEQUENCE 6

5.5 Strike Empi (elbow)

6.1 Grabbing wrist with both hands

5.4 Pull towards your left releasing
attackers grip

6.2 Rotate hand towards your left,
pressing both palms together

6.3 Stepping back, push against arm
to release

6.4 Lean back

SEQUENCE 7

6.5 Kick to stomach

7.1 Attacked from behind

7.2 Bear hug

7.3 Lifting knee

7.4 Striking to attackers foot with heel

7.5 Lean head back striking to face

7.6 Raise right hand

7.7 Strike to groin with hand

7.8 Lean forward and strike to groin with heel

SEQUENCE 8

8.1 Attacker positioning himself

8.2 Attacker grabbing from behind

8.3 Raising arm to strike

Section 1 : Basic Techniques – Self Defence

8.4 Strike Ippon Ken (one knuckle fist)

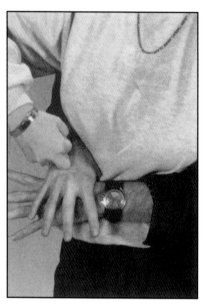

8.4A Close up

8.5 Ready to strike

8.6 Strike Empi (elbow)

8.7 Ready to strike

8.8 Strike to groin with open hand

SEQUENCE 9

9.1 Attacker positioning himself

9.2 Grab from behind under arms

9.3 Grabbing and pulling attackers little finger

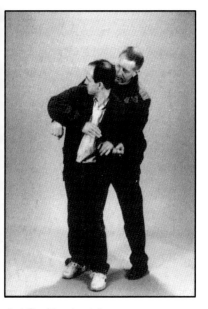

9.4 Position to strike

9.5 Strike Empi (elbow)

9.6 Turn positioning to strike

SELF DEFENCE

9.7 Strike to groin

10.1 Attacker grabbing lapel

10.2 Hold hand down on lapel. Attack to eyes

10.3 Using both hands, twist attackers wrist towards your left side

10.4 Making sure both thumbs are placed on attackers hand

10.5 Step back, pulling attacker down with wrist lock

SEQUENCE 11

10.6 Strike with kick

11.1 Attacker grabbing hold of hair
from the front

11.2 Using both hands press
attackers hands down

SEQUENCE 12

11.3 Pull attackers hand down and
away

11.4 Kick to groin

12.1 Attacker grabbing wrist

12.2 Grab attackers wrist

12.3 Spin attackers arm in an outward motion

12.4 Stepping underneath attackers arm, and positioning towards arm lock

SEQUENCE 13

12.5 Push attacker down with left hand on shoulder

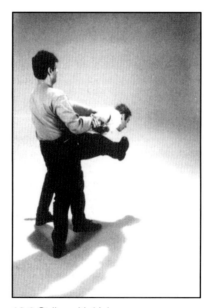

12.6 Strike with kick

13.1 Attacker grabbing hold of wrist

13.2 Grab hold of attackers wrist

13.3 Spin attackers arm in an inwards motion (anti-clockwise)

13.3A Start to turn your body in an anti-clockwise motion

13.4 Turn your body

13.5 Create an arm lock

13.6 Place left hand behind attackers elbow

Section 1 : Basic Techniques – Self Defence

SELF DEFENCE

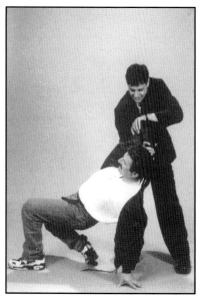

13.7 Push attacker down

13.8 Ready to strike

13.9 Strike Shuto (Knife hand strike)

SEQUENCE 14

14.1 Hand shake

14.2 Attacker squeezing hand

14.3 Place left hand on elbow joint and push. Twist your right hand clockwise with elbow and wrist lock

SEQUENCE 15

14.4 Strike with kick

15.1 Handshake

15.2 Turn attackers palm upwards turning body side on

15.3 Come over attackers arm, grabbing hold of your lapel

15.4 Pulling attackers palm down. Putting pressure on attackers elbow joint

15.5 Strike Empi (elbow)

SEQUENCE 16

15.6 Strike to groin

16.1 Handshake

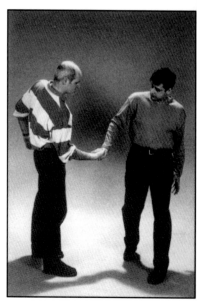

16.2 Turn body and twist attackers hand underneath

16.3 Whilst turning full circle

16.4 Grab attackers hand with other hand

16.5 Strike with kick

SEQUENCE 17

17.1 Attacker grabbing from side

17.2 Grab hold of attackers arm

17.3 Ready to strike

17.4 Strike to face with right hand

17.5 Ready to strike

17.6 Lean down and strike to groin

SELF DEFENCE

SEQUENCE 18

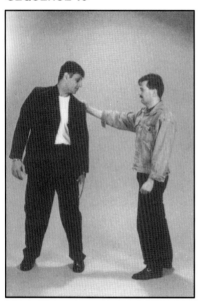

18.1 Attacker grabbing from side

18.2 Ready to strike

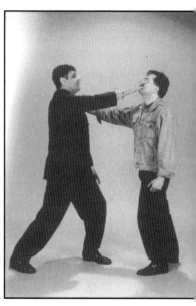

18.3 Strike to face with right hand

18.4 Drop left hand

18.5 Block Age Uke (Upper Rising Block) to disengage

18.6 With right hand grabbing hold of attackers head

18.7 Pull attackers head down. Strike
with Hiza (knee)

*"Know yourself first
and then others"*

KUMITE
Sparring

Kumite (sparring) is divided into various categories of pre-arranged sparring. Namely: Gohon Kumite – five-attack sparring Sanbon Kumite – three-attack sparring, Kihon Ippon Kumite – basic one-attack sparring, Kaeshi Ippon Kumite – basic one-attack sparring (with returning step counter-attack), Jiyu Ippon Kumite – semi free one-attack sparring, Okuri Jiyu Ippon Kumite (as Jiyu Ippon, but with a second free attack) and finally Jiyu Kumite – freestyle, which enables the Karate-Ka to use freely any of the aforementioned techniques against their opponent without warning. At all times, you should remember to take into consideration the essence of Karate-Do, i.e. "Karate ni sentanashi", there is no first attack in Karate.

GOHON KUMITE : *5 Attack Sparring*

Gohon Kumite is the most basic form of sparring in Karate. This Kumite is composed of five stepping attacks, five defensive blocks and a counter attack with KIAI (Shout). At this stage of your training your basics are now practised with the aid of a partner and this helps to develop your timing and distancing.

. YOI

2. The person attacking steps back into Gedan Barai

3. Hidari Age Uke | Migi Oi Zuki

. Migi Age Uke | Hidari Oi Zuki

5. Hidari Age Uke | Migi Oi Zuki

6. Migi Age Uke | Hidari Oi Zuki

. Hidari Age Uke | Migi Oi Zuki

8. Right Gyaku Zuki counter attack with **KIAI**

Both pulling up into YOI

GO HON KUMITE : CHUDAN

1. YOI

2. The person attacking steps back into Gedan Barai

3. Migi Oi Zuki | Hidari Soto Ude Uke

4. Hidari Oi Zuki | Migi Soto Ude Uke

5. Migi Oi Zuki | Hidari Soto Ude Uke

6. Hidari Oi Zuki | Migi Soto Ude Uke

7. Migi Oi Zuki | Hidari Soto Ude Uke

8. Right Gyaku Zuki counter attack with **KIAI**

Both pulling up into YOI

. YOI

2. The person attacking steps back into Zenkutsu Dachi

3. Hidari Gedan | Migi Mae
   Barai | Geri

. Migi Gedan | Hidari Mae
   Barai | Geri

5. Hidari Gedan | Migi Mae
   Barai | Geri

6. Migi Gedan | Hidari Mae
   Barai | Geri

7. Hidari Gedan | Migi Mae
   Barai | Geri

8. Right Gyaku Zuki counter attack with **KIAI**

Both pulling up into YOI

SANBON KUMITE : *3 Attack Sparring*

SANBON Kumite is a 3-attack sparring combination. The procedure is almost identical to Gohon Kumite, with the exception that the attack levels may be Jodan, Chudan or Mae Geri, or any combination of the three (as illustrated in this section). The defensive sequence is Age Uke, Soto Ude Uke and Gedan Barai with Gyaku Zuki as the counter-attack.

1. YOI

2. The person attacking steps back into Gedan Barai

3. Oi Zuki Jodan | Hidari Age Uke

4. Oi Zuki Chudan | Migi Soto Ude Uke

5. Mae Geri Chudan | Hidari Gedan Barai

6. Right Gyaku Zuki counter attack with **KIAI**

7. Yame

Both pulling up into YOI

KIHON IPPON KUMITE : *Basic 1 Attack Sparring*

Kihon Ippon Kumite is a combination of predetermined attacks and defences. The defender can now execute pre-arranged blocks by moving at different angles. These combinations should be practised both sides.

KIHON IPPON KUMITE : SET 1

JODAN

| 1. YOI | Hidari Gedan Barai | 2. Hidari Jodan Age Uke | Migi Jodan Oi Zuki | 3. Migi Chudan Gyaku Zuki | |

CHUDAN

| 1. Hidari Gedan Barai | YOI | 2. Migi Chudan Oi Zuki | Hidari Chudan Soto Ude Uke | 3. Migi Chudan Oi Zuki | Migi Chudan Gyaku Zuki |

MAE GERI

| 1. YOI | Hidari Zenkutsu Dachi | 2. Hidari Gedan Barai | Migi Chudan Mae Geri | 3. Migi Chudan Gyaku Zuki | Migi Zenkutsu Dachi |

KEKOMI

| . Hidari Zenkutsu Dachi | Yoi | 2. Migi Chudan Yoko Geri Kekomi | Hidari Chudan Soto Ude Uke | 3. Migi Chudan Gyaku Zuki |

MAWASHI GERI

| . Yoi | Hidari Zenkutsu Dachi | 2. Hidari Jodan Uchi Ude Uke (90°) | Migi Jodan Mawashi Geri | 3. Migi Chudan Gyaku Zuki |

KIHON IPPON KUMITE : SET 2

JODAN

1. YOI | Hidari Gedan Barai

2. Intermediate movement

3. Hidari Jodan Tate Shuto Uke | Migi Jodan Oi Zuki

4. Migi Jodan Shuto Uchi

CHUDAN

1. YOI | Hidari Gedan Barai

2. Uchi Uke | Oi Zuki

3. Gyaku Zuki | Oi Zuki

MAE GERI

1. YOI	Zenkutsu Dachi	2. Kaki Uke	Mae Geri	3. Gyaku Zuki

KEKOMI

1. Hidari Zenkutsu Dachi	Yoi	2. Migi Chudan Yoko Geri Kekomi	Hidari Chudan Soto Ude Uke	3. Migi Chudan Gyaku Zuki

MAWASHI GERI

1. Yoi	Hidari Zenkutsu Dachi	2. Hidari Jodan Uchi Ude Uke (90°)	Migi Jodan Mawashi Geri	3. Migi Chudan Gyaku Zuki

JODAN

1. Gedan Barai | YOI   2. Oi Zuki Jodan | Age Uke   3. Oi Zuki | Grab Arm

CHUDAN

4. Intermediate Movement   5. Yoko Empi | 1. YOI | Gedan Barai

2. Uchi Uke | Oi Zuki   3. Kizami Zuki | Oi Zuki   4. Gyaku Zuki |

MAE GERI

| 1. Hidari Zenkutsu Dachi | YOI | 2. Migi Chudan Mae Geri | Hidari Kaki Uke | 3. Migi Zenkutsu Dachi | Hidari Jodan Uraken Uchi |

| 4. Migi Zenkutsu Dachi | Migi Chudan Gyaku Zuki |

KEKOMI

| 1. Hidari Zenkutsu Dachi | YOI | 2. Migi Chudan Yoko Geri Kekomi | Hidari Chudan Soto Ude Uke | 3. Migi Chudan Gyaku Zuki |

MAWASHI GERI

1. YOI | Hidari Zenkutsu Dachi

2. Hidari Jodan Uchi Ude Uke (90°) | Migi Jodan Mawashi Geri

3. Migi Chudan Gyaku Zuki

JODAN

1. Yoi / Gedan Barai   2. Intermediate Move   3. Te Osai Uke   4. Mawashi Empi

CHUDAN

1. Yoi / Gedan Barai   2. Shuto Uke   3. Kizami Mawashi Geri   4. Nukite Chudan

MAE GERI

1. Yoi / Zenkutsu Dachi   2. Sukui Uke   3. Gyaku Zuki

KEKOMI

1. Zenkutsu Dachi / Yoi   2. Kake Uke   3. Jodan Haito Uchi

MAWASHI GERI

1. Zenkutsu Dachi / Yoi   2. Shuto Morote Uke   3. Intermediate Move   4. Morote Yoko Empi

KIHON IPPON KUMITE (Basic 1 Attack Sparring) : SET 5

JODAN

1. Yoi / Gedan Barai

2. Haishu Juji Uke

3. Mawashi Geri

4. Intermediate Move

5. Ushiro Mawashi

CHUDAN

1. Gedan Barai

2. Empi Uke (Kiba Dachi)

3. Intermediate Move

4. Ushiro Mawashi Empi

MAE GERI

1. Yoi / Zenkutsu Dachi

2. Gedan Barai

3. Shuto Uke
(Neko Ashi Dachi)

4. Jodan Empi

KEKOMI

1. Yoi / Gedan Barai   2. Gedan Barai   3. Turn   4. Haito Uchi

MAWASHI GERI

1. Yoi / Zenkutsu Dachi   2. Intermediate Move   3. Soto Uke   4. Intermediate Move

5. Shuto Uchi

A young Sensei practicing with his older brother Bhupinder Sahota who is an 8 Dan in Tai Kwon-Do and Chief Instructor of Global (ITF) Institutes

The Shotokan Karate Handbook – Beginner to Black Belt

JODAN

1. Jiyu Dachi

2. Hidari Jodan | Migi Jodan
   Tate Shuto Uke | Oi Zuki

3. Migi Chudan Gyaku Zuki

CHUDAN

4. Hikite Gamae

1. Jiyu Dachi

2. Hidari Chudan | Migi Chudan
   Soto Ude Uke | Oi Zuki

3. Migi Chudan Gyaku Zuki

4. Hikite Gamae

Section 2 : Kumite – Jiyu Ippon Set 1

MAE GERI

1. Jiyu Dachi

2. Hidari Gedan Barai | Migi Chudan Mae Geri

3. Migi Chudan Gyaku Zuki

4. Hikite Gamae

KEKOMI

1. Jiyu Dachi

2. Migi Chudan Yoko Geri Kekomi | Hidari Chudan Soto Ude Uke

3. Hidari Chudan Kizami Mawashi Geri

4. Migi Chudan Gyaku Zuki

5. Hikite Gamae

MAWASHI GERI

1. Jiyu Dachi

2. Hidari Jodan | Migi Jodan
   Haiwan Uke | Mawashi Geri

3. Migi Chudan Gyaku Zuki

4. Hikite Gamae

USHIRO GERI

1. Jiyu Dachi

2. Intermediate| Movement

3. Migi Chudan | Kage Uke
   Ushiro Geri

4. | Hidari Chudan
   | Gyaku Zuki

5. | Hikite Gamae

JIYU IPPON KUMITE : SET 2

JODAN

1. Jiyu Dachi

2. Oi Zuki Jodan | Age Uki

3. Gyaku Zuki

CHUDAN

4. Hikite Gamae

1. Jiyu Dachi

2. Chudan Oi Zuki | Uchi Uke

3. Oi Zuki | Gyaku Zuki

4. Hikite Gamae

MAE GERI

1. Jiyu Dachi

2. Mae Geri | Gedan Barai

3. Gyaku Zuki

4. Hikite Gamae

KEKOMI

1. Jiyu Dachi

2. Migi Chudan Yoko Geri Kekomi | Hidari Chudan Soto Ude Uke

3. Hidari Chudan Kizami Mawashi Geri

4. Migi Chudan Gyaku Zuki

5. Hikite Gamae

MAWASHI GERI

1. Jiyu Dachi

2. Hidari Jodan Haiwan Uke | Migi Jodan Mawashi Geri

3. Migi Chudan Gyaku Zuki

USHIRO GERI

4. Hikite Gamae

1. Jiyu Dachi

2. Intermediate Movement

3. Migi Chudan Ushiro Geri | Kage Uke

4. | Hidari Chudan Gyaku Zuki

5. | Hikite Gamae

JODAN

| 1. Jiyu Dachi | 2. Migi Jodan Age Uke | Migi Jodan Oi Zuki | 3. Migi Chudan Kizami Mawashi Geri |

CHUDAN

| 4. Hidari Chudan Gyuku Zuki | 5. Hikite Gamae | 1. Jiyu Dachi |

| 2. Chudan Oi Zuki | Chudan Uchi Uke | 3. Kizami Zuki Jodan | 4. Gyaku Zuki Chudan |

CHUDAN

5. Hikite Gamae

MAE GERI

1. Jiyu Dachi

2. Migi Gedan Barai | Migi Chudan Mae Geri

3. Hidari Gyaku Tate Shuto

4. Migi Jodan Kizami Zuki

5. Hikite Gamae

KEKOMI

1. Jiyu Dachi

2. Migi Chudan Yoko Geri Kekomi | Hidari Chudan Soto Ude Uke

3. Hidari Chudan Kizami Mawashi Geri

KEKOMI

4. Migi Chudan Gyaku Zuki

5. Hikite Gamae

MAWASHI GERI

1. Jiyu Dachi

2. Hidari Jodan
   Haiwan Uke

Migi Jodan
Mawashi Geri

3. Migi Chudan Gyaku Zuki

4. Hikite Gamae

USHIRO GERI

1. Jiyu Dachi

2. Intermediate
   Movement

3. Migi Chudan | Kage Uke
   Ushiro Geri

4. | Hidari Chudan
     Gyaku Zuki

5. | Hikite Gamae

JODAN

1. Jiyu Dachi

2. Nagashi Uke

3. Haito Uchi

4. Hikite Gamae

CHUDAN

1. Jiyu Dachi

2. Gyaku Shuto Uke

3. Uraken Uchi

3. Snap Back

MAE GERI

1. Jiyu Dachi

2. Gedan Osae Uke

3. Intermediate Move

4. Nagashi Uke

5. Tate Shuto

6. Gyaku Zuki

7. Hikite Gamae

JIYU IPPON KUMITE (Semi Free 1 Step Sparring) : SET 4

KEKOMI

1. Jiyu Dachi

2. Gyaku Gedan Barai

3. Jodan Kizami Zuki

4. Hikite Gamae

MAWASHI GERI

1. Jiyu Dachi

2. Gyaku Zuki Chudan

3. Uraken Uchi Jodan

4. Snap back

1. Hikite Gamae

USHIRO GERI

1. Jiyu Dachi

2. Intermediate Move

3. Ushiro Geri | Gyaku Gedan Barai

4.   Kizami Zuki Jodan

5.   Gyaku Zuki

6. Hikite Gamae

JIYU IPPON KUMITE (Semi Free 1 Step Sparring) : SET 5

JODAN

1. Jiyu Dachi

2. Migi Jodan Oi Zuki

Hidari Tobi Te Osae Uke Migi Jodan Uraken Uchi

3. Jiyu Dachi

CHUDAN

1. Jiyu Dachi

2. Migi Chudan Oi Zuki | Migi Gyaku Gedan Barai

3. Migi Jodan Ushiro Mawashi Geri

4. Migi Ashi Barai

5. Intermediate Move

6. Hidari Tate Shuto

7. Migi Gyaku Zuki

8. Hikite Gamae

MAE GERI

1. Jiyu Dachi

2. Migi Chudan Mae Geri

3. Hidari Chudan Sukui Uke

4. Intermediate Move

5. Migi Ashi Barai

6. Hidari Tate Shuto

7. Migi Gyaku Zuki

8. Hikite Gamae

KEKOMI

1. Jiyu Dachi

2. Hidari Kake Uke | Migi Chudan Yoko Geri Kekomi

3. Migi Jodan Gyaku Zuki

4. Pull down

5. Hidari Tate Shuto

6. Migi Gyaku Zuki

7. Hikite Gamae

MAWASHI GERI

1 Jiyu Dachi

2. Migi Jodan Soto Ude Uke | Migi Jodan Mawashi Geri

3. Migi Chudan Kizami Mawashi Geri

4. Migi Ashi Barai

5. Intermediate move

6. Intermediate move

7. Hidari Tate Shuto

8. Migi Gyaku Zuki

9. Hikite Gamae

USHIRO GERI

1. Jiyu Dachi

2. Migi Chudan | Migi Gyaku
   Ushiro Geri | Sukui Uke

3. Front View

4. Hidari Ashi Barai

5. Hidari Tate Shuto

6. Migi Gyaku Zuki

7. Hikite Gamae

"Do not think that Karate
is only in the Dojo"

KATA
Formal Exercise

Kata, which means formal exercise, consists of a set number of pre-determined moves which are designed to be performed in a set sequence against an imaginary attacker or attackers, armed and unarmed.

With this in mind the Karate-Ka should, through practise, not only understand his Kihon (basic) techniques but also be aware of the Bunkai (applications).

KATA : *Formal Exercise*

The majority of time Kata is practised alone to enable the the Karate-Ka his own time to visualise how these techniques would be effective in reality, but constant practise with a partner is also a must, to ascertain distance and timing when applying Kihon applications. Courtesy is shown throughout Karate and is always made apparent when practising Kata by the Karate-Ka beginning and ending with a bow (Rei).

Listed below are the ten elements of Kata as taught by Sensei Kanazawa

1. **Yoi No Kisin** – the spirit of getting ready. The concentration of will and mind against the opponent as a preliminary to the movements of the Kata.

2. **Inyo** – the active and passive. Always keeping in mind both attack and defence.

3. **Chikara No Kyojaku** – the manner of using strength. The degree of power used for each movement and position in Kata.

4. **Waza No Kankyu** – the speed of movement. The speed used for each movement and position in Kata

5. **Tai No Shinshuku** – the degree of expansion or contraction. The degree of expansion or contraction of the body in each movement and position in Kata.

6. **Kokyu** – breathing. Breath control related to the posture and movement in Kata.

7. **Tyakugan** – the aiming points. In Kata you must keep the purpose of the movement in mind.

8. **Kiai** – shouting. Shouting at set points in Kata to demonstrate the martial spirit.

9. **Keitai No Hoji** – correct positioning. Correct positioning in movement and stance.

10. **Zanshin** – remaining on guard. Remaining on guard at the completion of the Kata (i.e. back to "Yoi") until told to relax "Enoy".

To assist the Karate Ka in their performance of Kata throughout this section, directions have been illustrated by the arrow of the compass e.g.

TAIKYOKU SHODAN

20 MOVEMENTS
Predominantly the most basic of Katas taught to Karate students. The Kata is comprised of the first taught stance (Zenkutsu Dachi), block (Gedan Barai Uke) and attack (Oi Zuki) Although this is the first Kata that a Student learns it is one to which, after years of practising advanced Katas, one would always return to.

TAIKYOKU SHODAN

1. YOI

2. Intermediate movement

3. Hidari Gedan Barai

4. Migi Oi Zuki

5. Intermediate movement

6. Migi Gedan Barai

7. Hidari Oi Zuki

8. Intermediate movement

Hidari Gedan Barai

10. Migi Oi Zuki

11. Hidari Oi Zuki

12. Migi Oi Zuki **KIAI**

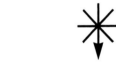

3. Intermediate
movement

14. Hidari Gedan Barai

15. Migi Oi Zuki

16. Intermediate
movement

17. Migi Gedan Barai

18. Hidari Oi Zuki

19. Intermediate
movement

20. Hidari Gedan Barai

21. Migi Oi Zuki

22. Hidari Oi Zuki

23. Migi Oi Zuki **KIAI**

24. Intermediate
movement

The Shotokan Karate Handbook – Beginner to Black Be

25. Hidari Gedan Barai

26. Migi Oi Zuki

27. Intermediate
movement

28. Migi Gedan Barai

29. Hidari Oi Zuki

30. Move left leg into
YAME

TAIKYOKU SHODAN

Application

1.

2.

3.

4.

5.

6.

The Shotokan Karate Handbook – Beginner to Black Be

HEIAN SHODAN: *Peaceful Mind Level 1*

1 MOVEMENTS

There are 5 Heian Katas to master with Heian Shodan being the first. This Kata now incorporates Shuto Uke, Age Uke and Tettsui Uchi, plus original movements from Taikyoku Shodan.

HEIAN SHODAN

1. Yoi

2. Intermediate movement

3. Zenkutsu Dachi
   Hidari Gedan Barai

4. Zenkutsu Dachi
   Migi Chudan Oi Zuki

5. Intermediate movement

6. Zenkutsu Dachi
   Migi Gedan Barai

7. Intermediate movement

8. Tettsui Uchi

. Zenkutsu Dachi
Hidari Chudan Oi Zuki

10. Intermediate
movement

11. Zenkutsu Dachi
Hidari Gedan Barai

12. Intermediate
movement

3. Zenkutsu Dachi
Migi Jodan Age Uke

14. Zenkutsu Dachi
Hidari Jodan Age Uke

15. Zenkutsu Dachi
Migi Jodan Age Uke
KIAI

16. Intermediate
movement

17. Zenkutsu Dachi
    Hidari Gedan Barai

18. Zenkutsu Dachi
    Migi Chudan Oi Zuki

19. Intermediate
    movement

20. Zenkutsu Dachi
    Migi Gedan Barai

21. Zenkutsu Dachi
    Hidari Oi Zuki

22. Intermediate
    movement

23. Zenkutsu Dachi
    Hidari Gedan Barai

24. Zenkutsu Dachi
    Migi Chudan Oi Zuki

25. Zenkutsu Dachi
    Hidari Chudan Oi Zuki

26. Zenkutsu Dachi
    Migi Chudan Oi Zuki
    KIAI

27. Front view

28. Intermediate
    movement

29. Kokutsu Dachi
    Hidari Chudan Shuto
    Uke

30. Intermediate
    movement

31. Kokutsu Dachi
    Migi Chudan Shuto
    Uke

32. Intermediate
    movement

33. Kokutsu Dachi
Migi Chudan Shuto
Uke

34. Intermediate
movement

35. Kokutsu Dachi
Hidari Chudan Shuto
Uke

36. Move left leg into
YAME

pplication

A.

2A.

A.

4A.

A.

6A.

Application

1B.

2B.

3B.

4B.

5B.

6B.

pplication

3.

HEIAN NIDAN: *Peaceful Mind Level 2*

26 MOVEMENTS
Heian Nidan now combines the new movements of Haiwan Uke, Ura Zuki, Uraken Uchi, Nukite, Mae Geri and Yoko Geri Keage into this level 2 Kata.

YOI

2. Intermediate movement

3. Kokutsu Dachi
Hidari Jodan Haiwan
Uke

4. Kokutsu Dachi
Hidari Ude Uke
Migi Ura Zuki

Kokutsu Dachi
Hidari Chudan Zuki

6. Intermediate movement

7. Kokutsu Dachi
Migi Jodan Haiwan Uke

8. Kokutsu Dachi
Migi Ude Uke
Hidari Ura Zuki

9. Kokutsu Dachi
   Migi Chudan Zuki

10. Koshi Gamae

11. Uraken Uke
    Yoko Geri Keage

12. Side view

13. Intermediate
    movement

14. Kokutsu Dachi
    Hidari Chudan Shuto
    Uke

15. Kokutsu Dachi
    Migi Chudan Shuto
    Uke

16. Kokutsu Dachi
    Hidari Chudan Shuto
    Uke

7. Te Osae Uke

18. Zenkutsu Dachi
Migi Chudan Shihon
Nukite **KIAI**

19. Intermediate
movement

20. Kokutsu Dachi
Hidari Chudan Shuto
Uke

1. Kokutsu Dachi
Migi Chudan Shuto
Uke

22. Intermediate
movement

23. Kokutsu Dachi
Migi Chudan Shuto
Uke

24. Kokutsu Dachi
Hidari Chudan Shuto
Uke

25. Intermediate
    movement

26. Intermediate
    movement

27. Front view

28. Zenkutsu Dachi
    Migi Uchi Uke Gyaku
    Hanmi

29. Front view

30. Migi Mae Geri

31. Front view

32. Zenkutsu Dachi
    Hidari Chudan
    Gyaku Zuki

3. Front view

34. Intermediate
movement

35. Front view

36. Zenkutsu Dachi
Hidari Chudan Uchi
Uke Gyaku Hanmi

37. Front view

38. Hidari Mae Geri

39. Zenkutsu Dachi
Migi Chudan Gyaku
Zuki

40. Front view

41. Intermediate
    movement

42. Front view

43. Zenkutsu Dachi
    Migi Chudan Morote
    Uke

44. Front view

45. Intermediate
    movement

46. Zenkutsu Dachi
    Hidari Gedan Barai

47. Intermediate
    movement

48. Intermediate
    movement

9. Migi Jodan Age Uke

50. Intermediate
    movement

51. Migi Gedan Barai

52. Intermediate
    movement

3. Hidari Jodan Age Uke
   KIAI

54. YAME

Application

1.

2.

3.

4.

5.

The Shotokan Karate Handbook – Beginner to Black Be

HEIAN SANDAN: *Peaceful Mind Level 3*

21 MOVEMENTS
Heian Sandan is performed in the line of a T. We now see the block Kosa Uke introduced into this Kata. This is a double block, whilst one arm blocks Gedan Barai Uke the other arm simultaneously blocks Uchi Uke.

1. YOI

2. Intermediate movement

3. Kokutsu Dachi
   Hidari Chudan
   Uchi Uke

4. Intermediate movemen

5. Heisoku Dachi
   Kosa Uke (Hidari
   Gedan Barai Uke)
   (Migi Chudan Uchi Uke)

6. Front view

7. Intermediate movement

8. Front view

Heisoku Dachi
Kosa Uke

10. Intermediate
movement

11. Kokutsu Dachi
Migi Chudan Uchi Uke

12. Intermediate
movement

3. Heisoku Dachi
Kosa Uke

14. Front view

15. Intermediate
movement

16. Heisoku Dachi
Kosa Uke

17. Intermediate movement

18. Kokutsu Dachi Hidari Chudan Morote Uke

19. Hidari Te Osae Uke

20. Zenkutsu Dachi Chudan Shihon Nukit

21. Intermediate movement

22. Intermediate movement

23. Kiba Dachi Hidari Chudan Tettsui Uchi

24. Zenkutsu Dachi Migi Chudan Oi Zuki KIAI

5. Heisoku Dachi
   Ryoken Koshi Gamae

26. Migi Fumikomi

27. Front view

28. Kiba Dachi
    Migi Empi Uke

9. Front view

30. Intermediate
    movement

31. Kiba Dachi
    Migi Jodan Uraken
    Uchi

32. Front view

33. Intermediate
movement

34. Hidari Fumikomi

35. Kiba Dachi
Hidari Empi Uke

36. Intermediate
movement

37. Kiba Dachi
Hidari Jodan Uraken
Uchi

38. Intermediate
movement

39. Migi Fumikomi

40. Front view

Kiba Dachi
Migi Empi Uke

42. Front view

43. Intermediate
movement

44. Front view

Kiba Dachi
Migi Jodan Uraken
Uchi

46. Intermediate
movement

47. Front view

48. Kiba Dachi
Migi Chudan Tate
Shuto Uke

49. Front view

50. Zenkutsu Dachi
Hidari Chudan Oi Zuki

51. Front view

52. Intermediate
movement

53. Intermediate
movement

54. Kiba Dachi
Migi Tate Zuki
Hidari Chudan Empi

55. Kiba Dachi
Hidari Tate Zuki
Migi Chudan Empi

56. Move right leg to
YAME

Application

2.

4.

6.

HEIAN YONDAN: *Peaceful Mind Level 4*

27 MOVEMENTS

Heian Yondan begins with virtually the same movement as Heian Nidan the difference being that the hands are open (Kaisho Haiwan Uke). Out of the Heian Katas this Kata has a wider number of kicks namely Mae Geri Yoko Geri Keage and Hiza Geri.

YOI

2. Intermediate movement

3. Kokutsu Dachi
   Kaisho Haiwan Uke

4. Intermediate movement

Kokutsu Dachi
Kaisho Haiwan Uke

6. Intermediate movement

7. Zenkutsu Dachi
   Gedan Juji Uke

8. Intermediate movement

9. Kokutsu Dachi
   Migi Chudan Morote
   Uke

10. Heisoku Dachi
    Koshi Gamae

11. Uraken Uchi
    Yoko Geri Keage

12. Zenkutsu Dachi
    Migi Mae Mawashi
    Empi Uchi

13. Top view

14. Heisoku Dachi
    Koshi Gamae

15. Uraken Uchi
    Yoko Geri Keage

16. Zenkutsu Dachi
    Hidari Mae Mawashi
    Empi Uchi

. Zenkutsu Dachi
Hidari Shuto Gedan
Barai
Migi Jodan Kaisho Age
Uke

18. Zenkutsu Dachi
Migi Jodan Shuto Uchi
Hidari Jodan Kaisho
Age Uke

19. Migi Jodan Mae Geri

20. Intermediate
movement
Te Osae Uke

. Kosa Dachi
Migi Chudan Uraken
Uchi **KIAI**

22. Intermediate
movement

23. Front view

24. Intermediate
movement

25. Front view

26. Kokutsu Dachi
    Chudan Kakiwake Uke

27. Front view

28. Migi Jodan Mae Geri

29. Zenkutsu Dachi
    Migi Chudan Oi Zuki

30. Zenkutsu Dachi
    Hidari Chudan Gyaku
    Zuki

31. Intermediate
    movement

32. Kokutsu Dachi
    Chudan Kakiwake Uk

3. Hidari Jodan Mae Geri

34. Zenkutsu Dachi
Hidari Chudan Oi Zuki

35. Zenkutsu Dachi
Migi Chudan Gyaku
Zuki

36. Intermediate
movement

7. Kokutsu Dachi
Hidari Chudan Morote
Uke

38. Front view

39. Intermediate
movement

40. Kokutsu Dachi
Migi Chudan Morote
Uke

HEIAN YONDAN

41. Intermediate
    movement

42. Kokutsu Dachi
    Hidari Chudan Morote
    Uke

43. Zenkutsu Dachi
    Morote Kubi Osae

44. Front view

45. Migi Hiza Geri Uchi
    KIAI

46. Front view

47. Intermediate
    movement

48. Kokutsu Dachi
    Hidari Chudan Shuto
    Uke

The Shotokan Karate Handbook – Beginner to Black Be

9. Kokutsu Dachi
Migi Chudan Shuto
Uke

50. Pull front leg back to
YAME

Application

1.

2.

3.

4.

5.

6.

HEIAN GODAN: *Peaceful Mind Level 5*

MOVEMENTS

This is the last of the Heian katas and we now see the introduction of some advanced techniques such as Jodan Kaisho Juji Uke, Gedan Juji Uke, Kagi Gamae (the flowing water technique) and also the practising of the skill of jumping over a "Bo".

HEIAN GODAN

1. YOI

2. Kokutsu Dachi
   Hidari Chudan Uchi
   Uchi

3. Kokutsu Dachi
   Migi Gyaku Zuki

4. Intermediate movemen

5. Heisoku Dachi
   Hidari Kagi Zuki

6. Kokutsu Dachi
   Migi Chudan Uchi Uke

7. Kokutsu Dachi
   Hidari Chudan Gyaku
   Zuki

8. Intermediate movemen

Heisoku Dachi
Migi Kagi Zuki

10. Kokutsu Dachi
    Migi Chudan Morote
    Uke

11. Intermediate
    movement

12. Zenkutsu Dachi
    Gedan Juji Uke

3. Intermediate
   movement

14. Zenkutsu Dachi
    Jodan Kaisho Juji Uke

15. Intermediate
    movement

16. Zenkutsu Dachi
    Chudan Osae Uke

HEIAN GODAN

17. Intermediate
movement
Tate Shuto Uke

18. Zenkutsu Dachi
Oi Zuki Chudan **KIAI**

19. Migi Fumikomi

20. Kiba Dachi
Migi Gedan Barai

21. Front view

22. Intermediate
movement

23. Kiba Dachi
Chudan Haishu Uke

24. Mikazuki Geri

Intermediate
movement

26. Kiba Dachi
    Migi Mawashi Empi
    Uchi

27. Intermediate
    movement

28. Kosa Dachi
    Migi Chudan Morote
    Uke

Renoji Dachi
Morote Jodan Ura
Zuki

30. Intermediate
    movement

31. Jumping over a Bo
    KIAI

32. Kosa Dachi
    Gedan Juji Uke

HEIAN GODAN

33. Intermediate movement

34. Zenkutsu Dachi Migi Chudan Morote Uke

35. Side view

36. Intermediate movements

37. Zenkutsu Dachi Hidari Nagashi Uke Migi Gedan Shuto Uchi

38. Intermediate movement

39. Kokutsu Dachi Manji Gamae

40. Intermediate movement

. Intermediate
movement

42. Heisoku Dachi
Manji Gamae

43. Intermediate
movement

44. Zenkutsu Dachi
Migi Nagashi Uke
Hidari Gedan Shuto
Uchi

. Kokutsu Dachi
Manji Gamae

46. Front leg is pulled up
into **YAME**

Applications

1.

2.

3.

4.

5.

6.

TEKKI SHODAN: *Horse Riding – Level 1*

riginally this Kata was
nown as Naihanchi which
as then renamed "Tekki"
y Sensei Funakoshi.
here are three Tekki
rms namely Shodan,
dan and Sandan. All the
ovements performed in
ekki are lateral with Kiba
achi being the dominant
ance. Nami Gaeshi
nside snapping foot
ock, returning wave) is
e of the most difficult
chniques to master in
is Kata.

1. YOI

2. Kata Yoi

3. Kosa Dachi

4. Fumikomi

5. Kiba Dachi
   Haishu Uke

6. Kiba Dachi
   Sokumen Empi

7. Kiba Dachi
   Koshi Gamae

8. Kiba Dachi
   Hidari Gedan Barai

Kiba Dachi
Migi Kagi Zuki

10. Kosa Dachi

11. Fumikomi

12. Kiba Dachi
Migi Uchi Uke

3. Intermediate
movement

14. Kiba Dachi
Hidari Jodan Nagashi
Uke

15. Kiba Dachi
Hidari Jodan Ura Zuki

16. Intermediate
movement

TEKKI SHODAN

17. Hidari Nami Ashi

18. Kiba Dachi
    Sokumen Hidari Uke

19. Migi Nami Ashi

20. Kiba Dachi
    Hidari Sokumen Uke

21. Kiba Dachi
    Koshi Gamae

22. Kiba Dachi
    Morote Zuki
    KIAI

23. Intermediate
    movement

24. Kiba Dachi
    Haishu Uke

25. Kiba Dachi
Sokumen Empi

26. Kiba Dachi
Koshi Gamae

27. Kiba Dachi
Migi Gedan Barai

28. Kiba Dachi
Hidari Kagi Zuki

29. Kosa Dachi

30. Fumikomi

31. Kiba Dachi
Hidari Uchi Uke

32. Intermediate
movement

33. Kiba Dachi
    Migi Jodan Nagashi
    Uke

34. Kiba Dachi
    Migi Jodan Ura Zuki

35. Intermediate
    movement

36. Migi Nami Ashi

37. Kiba Dachi
    Migi Sokumen Uke

38. Hidari Nami Ashi

39. Kiba Dachi
    Migi Sokumen Uke

40. Kiba Dachi
    Koshi Gamae

. Kiba Dachi
Morote Zuki
KIAI

42. Intermediate
movement

43. Intermediate
movement

44. **YAME**

TEKKI SHODAN

Applications

1.

2.

3.

BASSAI DAI: *To Storm a Fortress*

Bassai Dai is one of the
[old]est Katas and
[tra]nslated means "to storm
[a f]ortress", hence being a
[ver]y dynamic and powerful
[Kat]a. We now see the
[intr]oduction of Yama Zuki
[(V punch) along with
[Jo]dan Kekomi.

BASSAI DAI

1. YOI

2. Kata Yoi

3. Intermediate movement

4. Kosa Dachi
Migi Morote Uchi Ude Uke

5. Intermediate movement

6. Hidari Chudan Uchi Uke

7. Intermediate movement

8. Gyaku Hanmi
Gyaku Chudan Uchi Uke

Intermediate movement

10. Gyaku Hanmi
    Gyaku Chudan Soto
    Uke

11. Intermediate
    movement

12. Migi Chudan
    Uchi Uke

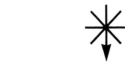

3. Gedan Sukui Uke

14. Intermediate
    movement
    Jodan Nagashi Uke

15. Intermediate
    movement

16. Migi Chudan Soto Uke

17. Intermediate
movement

18. Gyaku Hanmi
Gyaku Chudan Uchi
Uke

19. Intermediate
movement

20. Koshi Gamae

21. Hidari Chudan Tate
Shuto Uke

22. Migi Chudan Zuki

23. Intermediate
movement

24. Migi Chudan Uchi Uke

Hidari Chudan Zuki

26. Intermediate movement

27. Hidari Chudan Uchi Uke

28. Migi Chudan Shuto Uke

Hidari Chudan Shuto Uke

30. Migi Chudan Shuto Uke

31. Hidari Chudan Shuto Uke

32. Intermediate movement

BASSAI DAI

33. Migi Tsukami Uke
Hidari Soete

34. Intermediate
movement

35. Gedan Kekomi
KIAI

36. Hidari Chudan
Shuto Uke

37. Migi Chudan
Shuto Uke

38. Intermediate
movement

39. Front view

40. Intermediate
movement

The Shotokan Karate Handbook – Beginner to Black B

. Front view

42. Morote Age Uke
Heisoku Dachi

43. Front view

44. Intermediate
movement

. Front view

46. Chudan Tettsui
Hasami Uchi

47. Front view

48. Chudan Oi Zuki

BASSAI DAI

49. Front view

50. Intermediate movement

51. Zenkutsu Dachi Hidari Nagashi Uke Migi Gedan Shuto Uchi

52. Heisoku Dachi Manji Gamae

53. Intermediate movement Fumikomi Geri

54. Migi Gedan Barai

55. Intermediate movement

56. Hidari Chudan Haishu Uke

7. Front view

58. Migi Mikazuki Geri

59. Front view

60. Migi Mawashi Empi Uchi

1. Front view

62. Migi Gedan Barai
Hidari Soete

63. Hidari Gedan Barai
Migi Soete

64. Migi Gedan Barai
Hidari Soete

BASSAI DAI

65. Intermediate movement

66. Side view

67. Yama Zuki

68. Side view

69. Heisoku Dachi Koshi Gamae

70. Front view

71. Hidari Mikazuki Geri

72. Yama Zuki

. Side view

74. Intermediate movement

75. Migi Mikazuki Geri

76. Yama Zuki

7. Intermediate movement

78. Intermediate movement

79. Migi Gedan Sukui Uke

80. Intermediate movement

BASSAI DAI

81. Intermediate movement

82. Hidari Gedan Sukui Uke

83. Intermediate movement

84. Migi Chudan Shuto Uke

85. Intermediate movement Migi Chudan Shuto Uke

86. Hidari Chudan Shuto Uke **KIAI**

87. Intermediate movement

88. Yame

9. YAME

Applications

1A.

2A.

3A.

4A.

BASSAI DAI

Application

1B.

2B.

3B.

4B.

5B.

The Shotokan Karate Handbook – Beginner to Black B

"Spirit first –
Technique second"

JI'IN: *Temple Grounds*

The word Ji'in is believed to have come from the Jion temple. Katas Ji'in, Jion and Jitte are often grouped together as intermediate Katas. Repetition of timing and stances in this Kata enables the Karate-Ka to perfect their balance and timing.

YOI

2. Kata Yoi

3. Zenkutsu Dachi
Kosa Uke

4. Intermediate movement

Kokutsu Dachi
Manji Gamae

6. Intermediate movement

7. Kokutsu Dachi
Manji Uke

8. Intermediate movement

9. Zenkutsu Dachi
   Hidari Jodan Age Uke

10. Zenkutsu Dachi
    Migi Chudan Oi Zuki

11. Intermediate
    movement

12. Zenkutsu Dachi
    Migi Jodan Age Uke

13. Zenkutsu Dachi
    Hidari Chudan Oi Zuki

14. Intermediate
    movement

15. Zenkutsu Dachi
    Hidari Gedan Barai

16. Intermediate
    movement

7. Kiba Dachi
   Migi Jodan Shuto Uchi

18. Intermediate
    movement

19. Kiba Dachi
    Hidari Jodan Shuto
    Uchi

20. Intermediate
    movement

. Kiba Dachi
   Migi Jodan Shuto Uchi
   KIAI

22. Turning

23. Zenkutsu Dachi
    Kakiwake Uke

24. Migi Mae Geri

25. Zenkutsu Dachi
    Migi Chudan Oi Zuki

26. Zenkutsu Dachi
    Hidari Chudan Gyaku
    Zuki

27. Zenkutsu Dachi
    Kosa Uke

28. Front view

29. Zenkutsu Dachi
    Kakiwake Uke

30. Front view

31. Mae Geri

32. Zenkutsu Dachi
    Hidari Chudan Oi Zuk

3. Zenkutsu Dachi
   Migi Chudan Gyaku
   Zuki

34. Zenkutsu Dachi
    Kosa Uke

35. Intermediate
    movement

36. Kiba Dachi
    Migi Chudan Tettsui
    Uchi

7. Front view

38. Intermediate
    movement

39. Kiba Dachi
    Hidari Chudan Tettsui
    Uchi

40. Intermediate
    movement

41. Kiba Dachi
    Migi Chudan Tettsui
    Uchi

42. Intermediate
    movement

43. Zenkutsu Dachi
    Hidari Chudan Tate
    Shuto Uke

44. Zenkutsu Dachi
    Migi Chudan Gyaku
    Zuki

45. Hidari Chudan Zuki

46. Migi Mae Geri

47. Zenkutsu Dachi
    Migi Chudan Gyaku
    Zuki

48. Zenkutsu Dachi
    Kosa Uke

Intermediate
movement

50. Kiba Dachi
    Kosa Uke

51. Kiba Dachi
    Gedan Barai Uke

52. Intermediate
    movement

Kiba Dachi
Morote Chudan Kosa
Uke

54. Kiba Dachi
    Hidari Jodan Zuki

55. Kiba Dachi
    Migi Chudan Zuki
    KIAI

56. Yame

57. **YAME**

Applications

1.

1A.

2.

2A.

s Kata like Jion takes its
ne from the Jion
nple where martial arts
e taught. This Kata
sists of many of the
ic techniques taught
ier on, but these are
v performed in a strong
eful manner.

1. YOI

2. Kata Yoi

3. Intermediate movement

4. Zenkutsu Dachi
   Kosa Uke

5. Intermediate movement

6. Zenkutsu Dachi
   Kakiwake Uke

7. Migi Mae Geri

8. Zenkutsu Dachi
   Migi Chudan Zuki

. Zenkutsu Dachi
   Hidari Gyaku Zuki

10. Zenkutsu Dachi
    Migi Chudan Zuki

11. Intermediate
    movement

12. Zenkutsu Dachi
    Kakiwake Uke

3. Hidari Mae Geri

14. Zenkutsu Dachi
    Hidari Chudan Zuki

15. Zenkutsu Dachi
    Migi Chudan Gyaku
    Zuki

16. Zenkutsu Dachi
    Hidari Chudan Zuki

17. Intermediate movement

18. Zenkutsu Dachi
    Hidari Jodan Age Uke

19. Zenkutsu Dachi
    Migi Chudan Gyaku Zuki

20. Intermediate movement

21. Zenkutsu Dachi
    Migi Jodan Age Uke

22. Zenkutsu Dachi
    Hidari Chudan Gyaku Zuki

23. Intermediate movement

24. Zenkutsu Dachi
    Hidari Jodan Age Uke

Zenkutsu Dachi
Oi Zuki Chudan
KIAI

26. Intermediate
movement

27. Kokutsu Dachi
Manji Uke

28. Kiba Dachi
Migi Chudan Kagi Zuki

Front view

30. Intermediate
movement

31. Front view

32. Kokutsu Dachi
Manji Uke

33. Kiba Dachi
    Hidari Chudan Kagi
    Zuki

34. Intermediate
    movement

35. Zenkutsu Dachi
    Hidari Gedan Barai
    Uke

36. Intermediate
    movement

37. Kiba Dachi
    Migi Chudan Teisho
    Uchi

38. Front view

39. Intermediate
    movement

40. Kiba Dachi
    Hidari Chudan Teisho
    Uchi

41. Intermediate
movement

42. Kiba Dachi
Migi Chudan Teisho
Uchi

43. Intermediate
movement

44. Kokutsu Dachi
Manji Uke

45. Intermediate
movement

46. Heisoku Dachi
Jodan Morote Uke

47. Intermediate
movement

48. Kokutsu Dachi
Manji Uke

49. Intermediate
    movement

50. Heisoku Dachi
    Jodan Morote Uke

51. Intermediate
    movement

52. Heisoku Dachi
    Ryowan Gamae

53. Intermediate
    movement

54. Kosa Dachi
    Gedan Juji Uke

55. Zenkutsu Dachi
    Ryowan Gedan Barai
    Uke

56. Intermediate
    movement

7. Zenkutsu Dachi
   Ryowan Uchi Uke

58. Zenkutsu Dachi
    Jodan Juji Uke

59. Zenkutsu Dachi
    Migi Ura Zuki
    Hidari Age Uke

60. Zenkutsu Dachi
    Migi Jodan Nagashi
    Uke
    Hidari Chudan Zuki

1. Zenkutsu Dachi
   Migi Jodan Ura Zuki

62. Intermediate
    movement

63. Zenkutsu Dachi
    Hidari Uchi Uke

64. Zenkutsu Dachi
    Migi Chudan Oi Zuki

65. Intermediate
movement

66. Zenkutsu Dachi
Migi Chudan Uchi Uke

67. Zenkutsu Dachi
Hidari Chudan Oi Zuki

68. Intermediate
movement

69. Zenkutsu Dachi
Hidari Gedan Barai

70. Intermediate
movement
Fumikomi

71. Front view

72. Kiba Dachi
Migi Otoshi Uke

Front view

74. Intermediate
movement
Fumikomi

75. Kiba Dachi
Hidari Otoshi Uke

76. Intermediate
movement

Kiba Dachi
Migi Otoshi Uke
Fumikomi

78. Jodan Tsukami Uke

79. Intermediate

80. Kiba Dachi
Hidari Yumi Zuki

81. Jodan Tsukami Uke

82. Kiba Dachi
Migi Yumi Zuki
KIAI

83. **YAME**

84. **YAME**

85. **YAME**

plications

2.

4.

JITTE: *Ten Hands*

Jitte is also known as Jutte (10 movements). This Kata is from the Tomari region and includes some 27 movements. The majority of techniques practised are to defend against an attack from a "Bo".

Shizentai

2. Kata Yoi
Jiai No Kamae

3. Intermediate movement

4. Intermediate movement

Intermediate movement

6. Intermediate movement

7. Zenkutsu Dachi
Migi Tekubi Kake Uke

8. Intermediate movement

9. Intermediate movement

10. Zenkutsu Dachi
Teisho Morote Uke

11. Zenkutsu Dachi
Hidari Haito Uke

12. Intermediate
movement

13. Kiba Dachi
Migi Haito Uchi

14. Intermediate
movement

15. Kiba Dachi
Migi Teisho Uchi

16. Kiba Dachi
Hidari Teisho Uchi

Kiba Dachi
Migi Teisho Uchi

18. Intermediate
movement

19. Kosa Dachi
Jodan Juji Uke

20. Kiba Dachi
Ryowan Gedan
Kakiwake

Intermediate
movement

22. Kiba Dachi
Yama Kakiwake

23. Intermediate
movement
Fumikomi

24. Kiba Dachi
Yama Uke

JITTE

25. Intermediate
    movement
    Fumikomi

26. Kiba Dachi
    Yama Uke

27. Intermediate
    movement
    Fumikomi

28. Kiba Dachi
    Yama Uke
    KIAI

29. Intermediate
    movement

30. Shizentai
    Ryowan Gamae

31. Intermediate
    movement

32. Zenkutsu Dachi
    Migi Jodan Shuto Uk

The Shotokan Karate Handbook – Beginner to Black E

. Side view

34. Zenkutsu Dachi
    Morote Koko Dori

35. Side view

36. Intermediate
    movement

. Front view

38. Sagi Ashi Dachi
    Morote Jo Dori

39. Front view

40. Zenkutsu Dachi
    Morote Jo Zuki Dashi

41. Intermediate
movement

42. Front view

43. Zenkutsu Dachi
Morote Koko Dori

44. Front view

45. Zenkutsu Dachi
Morote Jo Zuki Dashi

46. Intermediate
movement

47. Kokutsu Dachi
Manji Uke

48. Intermediate
movement

. Kokutsu Dachi
   Manji Uke

50. Intermediate
    movement

51. Hidari Jodan Age Uke

52. Migi Jodan Age Uke

. Hidari Jodan Age Uke

54. Migi Jodan Age Uke
    KIAI

55. **YAME**

56. **YAME**

JITTE

Applications

1.

2.

3.

4.

5.

6.

ENPI: *Flying Swallow*

This Kata is also known as Wanshu. It is performed in the line of a T. It consists of 37 movements. This Kata translated means the flight of the swallow because of the combinations of irregular high and low movements.

1. YOI

2. Kata Yoi

3. Intermediate movement

4. Tachi Hiza
   Gedan Barai Uke

5. Intermediate movement

6. Shizentai
   Koshi Gamae

7. Zenkutsu Dachi
   Migi Gedan Barai Uke

8. Intermediate moveme

Kiba Dachi
Hidari Kagi Zuki

10. Intermediate
movement

11. Zenkutsu Dachi
Hidari Gedan Barai
Uke

12. Zenkutsu Dachi
Jodan Gyaku Age Zuki

. Intermediate
movement

14. Zenkutsu Dachi
Kami Tsukami

15. Migi Hiza Geri

16. Kosa Dachi
Migi Nagashi Uke
Hidari Otoshi Zuki

17. Ushiro Gedan Barai
Uke

18. Zenkutsu Dachi
Hidari Gedan Barai
Uke

19. Zenkutsu Dachi
Migi Jodan Age Zuki

20. Zenkutsu Dachi
Kami Tsukami

21. Migi Hiza Geri

22. Kosa Dachi
Nagashi Uke
Otoshi Zuki

23. Ushiro Gedan Barai
Uke

24. Zenkutsu Dachi
Hidari Gedan Barai
Uke

Intermediate
movement

26. Intermediate
movement

27. Kiba Dachi
Jodan Haishu Uke

28. Kataashi Dachi
Empi Uchi
KIAI

Intermediate
movement

30. Intermediate
movement

31. Kiba Dachi
Hidari Chudan Tate
Shuto Uke

32. Kiba Dachi
Migi Chudan Zuki

33. Kiba Dachi
    Hidari Chudan Zuki

34. Zenkutsu Dachi
    Hidari Gedan Barai

35. Zenkutsu Dachi
    Migi Jodan Gyaku Age
    Zuki

36. Intermediate
    movement

37. Kokutsu Dachi
    Migi Chudan Shuto
    Uke

38. Front foot pulling back

39. Kokutsu Dachi
    Hidari Chudan Shuto
    Uke

40. Kokutsu Dachi
    Chudan Gyaku Zuki

Kokutsu Dachi
Migi Chudan Shuto
Uke

42. Intermediate
movement

43. Zenkutsu Dachi
Hidari Gedan Barai

44. Zenkutsu Dachi
Migi Jodan Gyaku Age
Zuki

Zenkutsu Dachi
Kami Tsukami

46. Hiza Geri

47. Kosa Dachi
Migi Nagashi Uke
Hidari Otoshi Zuki

48. Ushiro Gedan Barai
Uke

49. Zenkutsu Dachi
    Hidari Gedan Barai

50. Intermediate
    movement

51. Intermediate
    movement

52. Zenkutsu Dachi
    Migi Teisho Uke

53. Intermediate
    movement

54. Zenkutsu Dachi
    Teisho Kosa Uke

55. Intermediate
    movement

56. Zenkutsu Dachi
    Teisho Kosa Uke

Intermediate
movement

58. Zenkutsu Dachi
Teisho Kosa Uke

59. Intermediate
movement

60. Kokutsu Dachi
Migi Gedan Barai

Kiba Dachi
Morote Koko Gamae

62. Joho Kaiten Tobi
(Turning 360°)
KIAI

63. Kokutsu Dachi
Migi Chudan Shuto
Uke

64. Kokutsu Dachi
Hidari Chudan Shuto
Uke

65. **YAME**

Applications

2.

4.

KANKU DAI: *Viewing the sky*

This Kata is also known as Kushanku. It was from this Kata that Sensei Itosu took numerous movements to create the five Heian Katas, hence the perfecting of the Heians enables an easier understanding and ability to improve the Kata Kanku Dai.

Kanku means to view the sky and this derived from the first movement of the Kata. This was one of Sensei Funakoshi's favourite Katas.

YOI

2. Intermediate movement

3. Intermediate movement

4. Awase Kaisho Age Uke

Intermediate movement

6. Intermediate movement

7. Gedan Shuto Uke

8. Intermediate movement

9. Kokutsu Dachi
   Kaisho Haiwan Uke

10. Intermediate
    movement

11. Kokutsu Dachi
    Kaisho Haiwan Uke

12. Intermediate
    movement

13. Shizentai
    Hidari Chudan Tate
    Shuto Uke

14. Shizentai
    Migi Chudan Zuki

15. Intermediate
    movement

16. Migi Chudan Uchi Uke

Shizentai
Hidari Chudan Zuki

18. Intermediate
movement

19. Hidari Chudan Uchi
Uke

20. Intermediate
movement

Kataashi Dachi
Koshi Gamae

22. Uraken Uchi
Yoko Geri Keage

23. Side view

24. Intermediate
movement

KANKU DAI

25. Kokutsu Dachi
    Hidari Chudan Shuto
    Uke

26. Kokutsu Dachi
    Migi Chudan Shuto
    Uke

27. Kokutsu Dachi
    Hidari Chudan Shuto
    Uke

28. Te Osae Uke

29. Zenkutsu Dachi
    Migi Chudan Shihon
    Nukite
    KIAI

30. Intermediate
    movement

31. Gyaku Hanmi
    Migi Jodan Shuto Uchi

32. Front view

. Migi Jodan Mae Geri

34. Front view

35. Intermediate
movement

36. Kokutsu Dachi
Manji Gamae

7. Zenkutsu Dachi
Hidari Nagashi Uke
Migi Gedan Shuto
Uchi

38. Intermediate
movement

39. Renoji Dachi
Gedan Barai Uke

40. Intermediate
movement

41. Migi Jodan Shuto Uchi
Hidari Kaisho Age Uke

42. Migi Jodan Mae Geri

43. Intermediate
movement

44. Kokutsu Dachi
Manji Gamae

45. Zenkutsu Dachi
Hidari Nagashi Uke
Migi Gedan Shuto
Uchi

46. Intermediate
movement

47. Renoji Dachi
Gedan Barai Uke

48. Intermediate
movement

Uraken Uke
Hidari Yoko
Geri Keage

50. Zenkutsu Dachi
Mae Mawashi Empi

51. Arm view

52. Uraken Uchi
Migi Yoko Geri Keage

Zenkutsu Dachi
Mae Mawashi Empi

54. Intermediate
movement

55. Kokutsu Dachi
Hidari Chudan Shuto
Uke

56. Kokutsu Dachi
Migi Chudan Shuto
Uke

57. Intermediate
movement

58. Kokutsu Dachi
Migi Chudan Shuto
Uke

59. Kokutsu Dachi
Hidari Chudan Shuto
Uke

60. Intermediate
movement

61. Migi Jodan Shuto Uchi
Hidari Kaisho Age Uke

62. Migi Jodan Mae Geri

63. Intermediate
movement

64. Front view

Kosa Dachi
Migi Chudan Uraken
Uchi

66. Front view

67. Zenkutsu Dachi
    Migi Chudan Uchi Uke

68. Zenkutsu Dachi
    Hidari Chudan Gyaku
    Zuki

Zenkutsu Dachi
Migi Chudan Zuki

70. Intermediate
    movement

71. Migi Morote Ura Zuki
    Hiza Gamae

72. Intermediate
    movement

KANKU DAI

73. Kokutsu Dachi
Awase Gedan Shuto
Uke

74. Side view

75. Kokutsu Dachi
Migi Chudan Shuto
Uke

76. Intermediate
movement

77. Zenkutsu Dachi
Hidari Chudan Uchi
Uke

78. Zenkutsu Dachi
Migi Chudan Gyaku
Zuki

79. Intermediate
movement

80. Zenkutsu Dachi
Migi Chudan Uchi Uk

Hidari Gyaku Zuki

82. Migi Chudan Zuki

83. Ryoken Koshi Gamae

84. Uraken Uchi
    Yoko Geri Keage

Intermediate
movement

86. Kokutsu Dachi
    Hidari Chudan Shuto
    Uke

87. Zenkutsu Dachi
    Te Osae Uke
    Migi Chudan Shihon
    Nukite

88. Intermediate
    movement

89. Intermediate movement

90. Kiba Dachi
Hidari Jodan Uraken Uchi

91. Intermediate movement

92. Kiba Dachi
Hidari Chudan Tetts Uchi

93. Kiba Dachi
Sokumen Empi Uchi

94. Kiba Dachi
Ryoken Koshi Gamae

95. Migi Gedan Barai

96. Intermediate movement

7. Front view

98. Kiba Dachi
 Ryo Ude Mawashi Uke

99. Kiba Dachi
 Migi Otoshi Zuki

100. Intermediate
 movement

01. Shizentai
 Jodan Kaisho Juji
 Uke

102. Front view

103. Intermediate
 movement

104. Intermediate
 movement

KANKU DAI

105. Moto Dachi
Juji Gamae

106. Hidari Tobi Geri

107. Front view

108. Migi Tobi Geri

109. Side view

110. Zenkutsu Dachi
Migi Chudan Uraken
Uchi

111. **YAME**

112. **YAME**

3. Intermediate
movement

114. **YAME**

115. **YAME**

116. **YAME**

KANKU DAI

Applications

1.

2.

3.

GANKAKU: *Crane on a Rock*

This Kata was previously known as Chinto. It was renamed by Sensei Funakoshi and translated means "Crane on a rock". This resembles a crane standing on one foot on a rock ready to pounce on its prey. The performance line of this Kata is a straight line.

GANKAKU

1. YOI

2. Intermediate movement

3. Kokutsu Dachi
   Sokumen Awase Uke

4. Intermediate moveme

5. Intermediate movement

6. Kokutsu Dachi
   Hidari Chudan Zuki

7. Kokutsu Dachi
   Migi Chudan Gyaku
   Zuki

8. Intermediate moveme

Kiba Dachi
Migi Gedan Barai
Fumikomi Geri

10. Front view

11. Moto Dachi
    Jodan Kaisho Juji Uke

12. Moto Dachi
    Morote Tsukami Uke

. Nidan Geri
   Migi Mae Tobi Geri

14. Hidari Mae Tobi Geri

15. Zenkutsu Dachi
    Gedan Juji Uke

16. Intermediate
    movement

GANKAKU

17. Zenkutsu Dachi
Gedan Juji Uke

18. Kokutsu Dachi
Awase Gedan Barai
Uke

19. Intermediate
movement

20. Kokutsu Dachi
Awase Gedan Shuto
Uke

21. Intermediate
movement

22. Zenkutsu Dachi
Shuto Kakiwake Uke

23. Intermediate
movement

24. Kiba Dachi
Haito Kakiwake Uke

The Shotokan Karate Handbook – Beginner to Black B

Intermediate movement

26. Ryowan Shizentai

27. Kokutsu Dachi Manji Uke

28. Side view

Kokutsu Dachi Manji Uke

30. Intermediate movement

31. Kokutsu Dachi Manji Uke

32. Intermediate movement

33. Gedan Juji Uke
    Kata Hiza Dachi

34. Intermediate
    movement

35. Kiba Dachi

36. Intermediate
    movement

37. Ryowan Shizentai

38. Ryoken Koshi Gamae

39. Migi Empi Uke

40. Hidari Empi Uke

Intermediate
movement

42. Kosa Dachi
    Ryowan Uchi Uke

43. Intermediate
    movement

44. Intermediate
    movement

Tsuru Ashi Dachi
Manji Gamae

46. Intermediate
    movement

47. Tsuru Ashi Dachi
    Ryoken Koshi Gamae

48. Uraken Uchi
    Yoko Geri Keage

49. Intermediate
    movement

50. Zenkutsu Dachi
    Chudan Oi Zuki
    KIAI

51. Intermediate
    movement

52. Tsuru Ashi Dachi
    Manji Gamae

53. Tsuru Ashi Dachi
    Ryoken Koshi Gamae

54. Uraken Uchi
    Yoko Geri Keage

55. Kiba Dachi
    Migi Sokumen Zuki

56. Intermediate
    movement

. Tsuru Ashi Dachi
  Manji Gamae

58. Intermediate
    movement

59. Tsuru Ashi Dachi
    Ryoken Koshi Gamae

60. Uraken Uchi
    Yoko Geri Keage

. Front view

62. Kiba Dachi
    Sokumen Zuki

63. Kiba Dachi
    Jodan Shuto Uke

64. Zenkutsu Dachi
    Age Empi Uchi

65. Intermediate
movement

66. Zenkutsu Dachi
Koshi Gamae

67. Intermediate
movement

68. Intermediate
movement

69. Tsuru Ashi Dachi
Ryoken Koshi Gamae

70. Uraken Uchi
Yoko Geri Keage

71. Front view

72. Intermediate
movement

Zenkutsu Dachi
Chudan Oi Zuki
KIAI

74. Intermediate
movement

75. **YAME**

•plications

.

2A.

GANKAKU

3A.

4A.

5A.

6A.

Applications

1B.

2B.

4B.

6B.

HANGETSU: *Half Moon (or Wide Hour Glass)*

This Kata translated means "Half Moon" because of the semi circular hand and foot movements used. The performance line of this Kata is cross shaped.

YOI

2. Intermediate movement

3. Hangetsu Dachi
   Hidari Chudan Uchi Uke

4. Hangetsu Dachi
   Migi Chudan Gyaku
   Zuki

Intermediate movement

6. Hangetsu Dachi
   Migi Chudan Uchi Uke

7. Hangetsu Dachi
   Hidari Chudan Gyaku
   Zuki

8. Intermediate movement

HANGETSU

9. Hangetsu Dachi
Hidari Chudan Uchi Uke

10. Hangetsu Dachi
Migi Chudan Gyaku
Zuki

11. Intermediate
movement

12. Hangetsu Dachi
Morote Yoko Ken Ate

13. Hangetsu Dachi
Morote Ippon Ken

14. Intermediate
movement

15. Intermediate
movement

16. Hangetsu Dachi
Kaisho Yama Uke

. Intermediate
movement

18. Hangetsu Dachi
Ryowan Gedan Shuto
Uke

19. Intermediate
movement

20. Hangetsu Dachi
Kaisho Kosa Uke
(Hidari Seiryuto Uke
Migi
Haito
Uke)
KIAI

. Front view

22. Intermediate
movement
Migi Tsukami Uke

23. Front view

24. Hangetsu Dachi
Kaisho Kosa Uke
(Migi Seiryuto Uke
Hidari
Haito
Uke)

25. Intermediate
movement

26. Hungetsu Dachi
Kaisho Kosa Uke
(Hidari Seiryuko Uke
Migi
Haito
Uke)

27. Intermediate
movement

28. Intermediate
movement

29. Hangetsu Dachi
Migi Chudan Uchi Uke

30. Hangetsu Dachi
Hidari Chudan Gyaku
Zuki

31. Hangetsu Dachi
Migi Chudan Zuki

32. Intermediate
movement

The Shotokan Karate Handbook – Beginner to Black Be

Hangetsu Dachi
Hidari Chudan Uchi
Uke

34. Migi Gyaku Zuki

35. Hangetsu Dachi
    Hidari Chudan Zuki

36. Intermediate
    movement

. Migi Chudan Uchi Uke

38. Hidari Gyaku Zuki

39. Migi Chudan Zuki

40. Intermediate
    movement

41. Intermediate
    movement

42. Hidari Engetsu Uke

43. Intermediate
    movement

44. Kokutsu Dachi
    Chudan Uraken Uch

45. Hanmi Sashi Ashi

46. Hidari Mae Geri
    Hidari Hikite

47. Side view

48. Hangetsu Dachi
    Hidari Gedan Barai

Hangetsu Dachi
Migi Chudan Gyaku
Zuki

50. Hidari Age Uke

51. Intermediate
movement

52. Intermediate
movement

Intermediate
movement

54. Kokutsu Dachi
Chudan Uraken Uchi

55. Side view

56. Hanmi Sashi Ash

57. Migi Mae Geri
Migi Hikite

58. Hangetsu Dachi
Migi Gedan Barai

59. Hidari Chudan Gyaku
Zuki

60. Migi Age Uke

61. Intermediate
movement

62. Intermediate
movement

63. Intermediate
movement

64. Kokutsu Dachi
Chudan Uraken Uch

Migi Mikazuki Geri
KIAI

66. Zenkutsu Dachi
Migi Gedan Gyaku
Zuki

67. Intermediate
movement

68. Neko Ashi Dachi
Teisho Awase Gedan
Uke

YAME

HANGETSU

Application

1.

2.

3.

4.

5.

6.

WANKAN: *A Proper Name*

Wankan originated from Matsumora but was later adopted by both Shotokan and Shito-Ryu styles. This Kata has only one Kiai and although it is one of the shortest katas, it is one of the most difficult to perfect.

1. YOI

2. Intermediate movement

3. Neko Ashi Dachi
Chudan Kakiwake Uke

4. Intermediate moveme

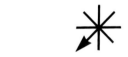

5. Neko Ashi Dachi
Chudan Kakiwake Uke

6. Awase Hasami Uke
Hiza Gamae

7. Neko Ashi Dachi

8. Neko Ashi Dachi

Intermediate movement

10. Zenkutsu Dachi
    Hidari Chudan Tate
    Shuto Uke

11. Zenkutsu Dachi
    Migi Chudan Zuki

12. Zenkutsu Dachi
    Hidari Chudan Gyaku
    Zuki

. Intermediate
 movement

14. Neko Ashi Dachi
    Koko Hiza Kuzushi

15. Intermediate
    movement

16. Zenkutsu Dachi
    Hidari Chudan Tate
    Shuto Uke

17. Zenkutsu Dachi
    Migi Chudan Zuki

18. Zenkutsu Dachi
    Hidari Chudan Gyaku
    Zuki

19. Intermediate
    movement

20. Neko Ashi Dachi
    Koko Hiza Kuzushi

21. Intermediate
    movement

22. Zenkutsu Dachi
    Hidari Chudan Tate
    Shuto Uke

23. Zenkutsu Dachi
    Migi Chudan Zuki

24. Zenkutsu Dachi
    Hidari Chudan Gyaku
    Zuki

Intermediate movement

26. Kiba Dachi Yoko Tettsui Uchi

27. Hidari Mae Geri

28. Hidari Chudan Zuki

Migi Mae Geri

30. Zenkutsu Dachi Migi Chudan Zuki

31. Hidari Mae Geri

32. Zenkutsu Dachi Hidari Chudan Zuki

33. Intermediate movement

34. Fudo Dachi Yama Zuki **KIAI**

35. Intermediate movement

36. **YAME**

Applications

1.

2.

plications

4.

6.

8.

*"Karate is like hot water –
if you do not give it heat constantly
it will again become cold"*

Preparing for Kumite Final 1978

GENERAL
INFORMATION

**Traditional International Shotokan Karate Association
(TISKA) Grade and Belt Order**

Grading Syllabuses

TISKA Club Photographs

English – Japanese Numbering

Glossary

Oath of the Dojo

TISKA GRADE AND BELT ORDER

GRADES	BELT COLOUR
BEGINNER	WHITE BELT
10th KYU	BLUE BELT
9th KYU	RED BELT
8th KYU	ORANGE BELT
7th KYU	YELLOW BELT
6th KYU Intermediate	YELLOW WITH GREEN TAG
6th KYU	GREEN BELT
5th KYU Intermediate	GREEN WITH PURPLE TAG
5th KYU	PURPLE BELT
4th KYU Intermediate	PURPLE WITH WHITE TAG
4th KYU	PURPLE WITH ONE WHITE STRIPE
3rd KYU Intermediate	PURPLE ONE WHITE STRIPE WITH BROWN TAG
3rd KYU	BROWN BELT
2nd KYU Intermediate	BROWN WITH WHITE TAG
2nd KYU	BROWN WITH ONE WHITE STRIPE
1st KYU Intermediate	BROWN ONE WHITE STRIPE WITH RED TAG
1st KYU	BROWN WITH ONE RED STRIPE
SHODAN INT.	BROWN WITH ONE BLACK STRIPE
1st DAN	BLACK BELT

The intermediate gradings are for juniors under the age of 14 years.

10ᵗʰ KYU - BLUE BELT

...mmands during this examination will be given in English

...SICS

Technique	Stance	Procedure
Choku Zuki (straight punch)	Shizentai	Facing front
Gyaku Zuki (reverse punch)	Zenkutsu	Left and right side
Oi Zuki (stepping punch)	Zenkutsu	Forward and stepping back
Age Uke (upper block)	Zenkutsu	Forward and stepping back
Gedan Barai (downward block)	Zenkutsu	Forward and stepping back
Mae Geri (front kick)	Zenkutsu	On the spot

...MITE

...Ion Kumite	5 attack sparring – Jodan (upper) level only to count	
	Seniors no count	(see pages 52 – 53)
	Juniors to count	(see pages 52 – 53)

Sensei G. Sahota explaining the importance of basics to some of the youngest members of the association.

BASICS

No.	Technique	Stance	Procedure
5	Choku Zuki (straight punch)	Shizentai	Facing front
5	Gyaku Zuki (reverse punch)	Zenkutsu	Left and right side
5	Oi Zuki (stepping punch)	Zenkutsu	Forward turn the same bac
5	Age Uke (Upper block)	Zenkutsu	Forward and stepping back
5	Soto Ude Uke (outside block)	Zenkutsu	Forward and stepping back
5	Uchi Ude Uke (inside block)	Zenkutsu	Forward and stepping back
5	Gedan Barai (downward block)	Zenkutsu	Forward and stepping back
5	Uraken (Back Fist)	Zenkutsu	Forward turn the same bac
5	Mae Geri (front kick)	Zenkutsu	On the spot

KUMITE

Go Hon Kumite	Jodan Seniors no count (see pages 52 – 53) Juniors to count (see pages 52 – 53)

KATA

Taikyoku Shodan	1st Half only Seniors no count (see pages 87 – 92) Juniors to count (see pages 87 – 92)

8TH KYU - ORANGE BELT

BASICS

.	Technique	Stance	Procedure
	Gyaku Zuki	Zenkutsu	Left and right side
	Oi Zuki	Zenkutsu	Forward turn the same back
	Age Uke	Zenkutsu	Forward and stepping back
	Soto Ude Uke	Zenkutsu	Forward and stepping back
	Uchi Ude Uke	Zenkutsu	Forward and stepping back
	Gedan Barai	Zenkutsu	Forward and stepping back
	Uraken	Zenkutsu	Forward turn the same back
	Mae Geri	Zenkutsu	On the spot
	Yoko Geri Keage	Kiba	Forward turn the same back

KUMITE

Hon Kumite   Jodan & Chudan
                 Seniors no count   (see pages 52 – 54)
                 Juniors to count   (see pages 52 – 54)

KATA

Taikyoku Shodan   Seniors no count (see pages 87 - 92)
                    Juniors to count (see pages 87 - 92)

BASICS

No	Technique	Stance	Procedure
5	Gyaku Zuki	Zenkutsu	On the spot
5	Oi Zuki	Zenkutsu	Forward turn the same back
5	Age Uke	Zenkutsu	Forward and stepping back
5	Soto Ude Uke	Zenkutsu	Forward and stepping back
5	Uchi Uke	Zenkutsu	Forward and stepping back
5	Shuto Uke	Kokutsu	Forward and stepping back
5	Gedan Barai	Zenkutsu	Forward and stepping back
5	Uraken Uchi	Zenkutsu	Forward turn the same back
5	Mae Geri	Zenkutsu	Forward turn the same back
5	Yoko Geri Keage	Kiba Dachi	Forward turn the same back
5	Uraken	(from Jiyu Dachi)	

KUMITE

Go Hon Kumite	Jodan & Chudan	
	Seniors no count	(see pages 52 – 54)
	Juniors to count	(see pages 52 – 54)

KATA

Taikyoku Shodan   See pages 87 - 92

-      No count

6th KYU - GREEN BELT

BASICS

o	Technique	Procedure
	Gyaku Zuki	On the spot
	Sanbon Zuki	Forward turn the same back
	Age Uke	Forward and stepping back
	Soto Ude Uke	Forward and stepping back
	Uchi Uke	Forward and stepping back
	Gedan Barai	Forward and stepping back
	Shuto Uke	Forward and stepping back
	Uraken Uchi	Forward turn the same back
	Tettsui Uchi (as per Heian Shodan)	Forward turn the same back
	Mae Geri Gyaku Zuki	Forward turn the same back
	Yoko Geri Keage	Turn the same back
	Yoko Geri Kekomi	Turn the same back

From Jiyu Dachi

	Uraken	(Sliding forward)
	Gyaku Zuki	(Sliding forward)

KUMITE

Go Hon Kumite
Jodan, Chudan, Mae Geri

Heian Shodan

See pages 93 – 101

- Junior intermediate grades - to count up to first Kiai (half Kata)
- Senior and full grades - no count (full Kata)

- Plus any previous Kata

BASICS

No	Technique	Procedure
5	Mae Geri Sambon Zuki	Forward turn the same back
5	Age Uke	Forward and stepping back
5	Soto Ude Uke	Forward and stepping back
5	Uchi Uke	Forward and stepping back
5	Shuto Uke	Forward and stepping back
5	Nukite	Forward and stepping back
5	Gedan Barai	Forward and stepping back
5	Morote Uke	Forward and stepping back
5	Uraken	Forward turn the same back
5	Mae Geri Gyaku Zuki	Forward turn the same back
5	Mawashi Geri	Forward turn the same back
5	Kekomi from kiba dachi	Forward turn the same back
5	Yoko Geri Keage	Forward turn the same back

From Jiyu Dachi Stance

Uraken Gyaku Zuki	(sliding forward)

KUMITE

Sanbon Kumite   -   One Jodan, One Chudan, One Mae Geri,
Intermediate grade 1 side only to count
Full Grade and Seniors both sides no count

KATA

Heian Nidan   -   See pages 102 - 110

Senior and full grades - no count (full Kata)
Junior intermediate grades - to count up to first Kiai (half Kat
Plus any previous Kata

4ᵗʰ KYU - PURPLE WITH ONE WHITE STRIPE

ASICS

o	Technique	Procedure
	Mae Geri/Sanbon Zuki	Forward turn the same back
	Age Uke/Gyaku Zuki/Gedan Barai	Forward and stepping back
	Soto Ude Uke/Gyaku Zuki/Gedan Bari	Forward and stepping back
	Uchi Uke/Gyaku Zuki/Gedan Barai	Forward and stepping back
	Shuto Uke/Nukite /Shuto Uke	Forward and stepping back
	Kosa Uke	Forward and stepping back
	Gedan Barai/Gyaku Zuki/Gedan Bari	Forward and stepping back
	Uraken/Gyaku Zuki/Gedan Barai	Forward turn the same back
	Mae Geri/Mawashi Geri (stepping forward)	Forward turn the same back
	Mae Geri/ Kekomi (stepping forward)	Forward turn the same back
	Keage (from kiba dachi)	Forward turn the same back

om Jiyu Dachi Stance

ie Geri, Uraken,	Stepping forward

UMITE

hon Ippon Kumite – Set 1.
Jodan, Chudan, Mae Geri, Kekomi and Mawashi Geri
(one side for tag)

ATA

ian Sandan (see pages 111 - 119)

Senior and full grades - no count (full Kata)
Junior intermediate grades - to count up to first Kiai (half Kata)
Plus any previous Kata

3rd KYU - BROWN BELT

BASICS

No	Technique	Procedure
5	Mae Geri/Sanbon Zuki	Forward turn the same back
5	Age Uke/Gyaku Zuki/Gedan Barai	Forward and stepping back
5	Soto Ude Uke/Gyaku Zuki/Gedan Barai	Forward and stepping back
5	Uchi Uke/Gyaku Zuki/Gedan Barai	Forward and stepping back
5	Shuto Uke/Nukite /Shuto Uke	Forward and stepping back
5	Gedan Barai/Gyaku Zuki/Gedan Barai	Forward and stepping back
5	Uraken/Gyaku Zuki/Gedan Bari	Forward turn the same back
5	Mae Geri/Mawashi Geri	Forward turn the same back
5	Mae Geri/ Kekomi	Forward turn the same back
5	Keage (from kiba dachi)	Forward turn the same back

Following Basics from Jiyu Dachi Stance

Mae Geri, Uraken, Gyaku Zuki	Stepping forward

KUMITE

Kihon Ippon Kumite -	Set 2. Jodan, Chudan, Mae Geri, Kekomi and Mawashi Geri Intermediate grade 1 side only to count Full Grade and Seniors both sides no count

KATA

Heian Yondan	(see pages 120 - 128) Junior intermediate grades - to count up to first Kiai (half kata) Senior and full grades - no count (full Kata) Plus any previous Kata

2nd KYU - BROWN BELT WITH ONE WHITE STRIPE

BASICS

No	Technique	Procedure
	Mae Geri/Sanbon Zuki	Forward turn the same back
	Age Uke/ /Gyaku Zuki/Gedan Barai	Forward and stepping back
	Soto Ude Uke/ Gyaku Zuki/Gedan Barai	Forward and stepping back
	Uchi Uke/Gyaku Zuki/Gedan Barai	Forward and stepping back
	Uraken Gyaku Zuki Gedan Barai	Forward and stepping back
	Shuto Uke/ Nukite/Shuto Uke	Forward and stepping back
	Gedan Barai/Gyaku Zuki/Gedan Barai	Forward and stepping back
	Uraken, Gyaku Zuki, Gedan Barai	Forward and stepping back
	Mae Geri/Mawashi Geri	Forward turn the same back
	Mae Geri/Kekomi	Forward turn the same back
	Keage (from kiba dachi)	Forward turn the same back
	Mae Geri/Kekomi	On the spot
	Ushiro Geri	Forward turn the same back

Following Basics from Jiyu Dachi Stance

Mae Geri, Uraken, Gyaku zuki
Gyaku Zuki, Mawashi Geri
Kekomi, Uraken

KUMITE

Jyu Ippon Kumite	-	**Set 1**
		Jodan, Chudan, Mae Geri, Kekomi, Mawashi Geri & Ushiro Geri
		Intermediate grade 1 side only to count
		Full Grade and Seniors both sides no count

KATA

Heian Godan   (see pages 129 - 136)

Junior intermediate grades - to count up to first Kiai (half kata)

Senior and full grades (full Kata)
Plus any previous Kata

1st KYU - BROWN BELT WITH ONE RED STRIPE

BASICS

No	Technique	Procedure
5	Mae Geri/Sanbon Zuki	Forward turn the same back
5	Age Uke/ Gyaku Zuki/Gedan Barai	Forward and stepping back
5	Soto Ude Uke/ Gyaku Zuki/Gedan Barai	Forward and stepping back
5	Uchi Uke/Kizami Zuki/Gyaku Zuki/Gedan Barai	Forward and stepping back
5	Shuto Uke/Kizami Mawashi Geri/Nukite/Shuto Uke	Forward and stepping back
5	Gedan Barai/Gyaku Zuki/Gedan Barai	Forward and stepping back
5	Uraken, Gyaku Zuki, Gedan Barai	Forward and stepping back
5	Mae Geri/Mawashi Geri/Uraken/Gyaku Zuki/Gedan Barai	Forward turn the same back
5	Mae Geri/Kekomi/Shuto Uke/Gyaku Zuki/Gedan Barai	Forward turn the same back
5	Keage (from kiba dachi)	Forward turn the same back
5	Mae Geri/Kekomi	On the spot
5	Ushiro Geri	Forward turn the same back

Following Basics from Jiyu Dachi Stance

Gyaku Zuki/Mawashi Geri	Stepping forward
Kekomi /Uraken	Stepping forward
Step up Ushiro Mawashi Geri (front foot)	

KUMITE

Jiyu Ippon Kumite	-	**Set 2.**
		Jodan, Chudan, Mae Geri, Kekomi, Mawashi Geri, Ushiro Geri
		Intermediate grade 1 side only to count
		Full Grade and Seniors both sides no count

KATA

Tekki Shodan

(see pages 137 - 144)

Junior intermediate grades - to count up to first Kiai (half kata

Senior and full grades (full Kata)
Plus any previous Kata

BROWN WITH BLACK STRIPE - SHODAN INT.

BASICS

Technique	Procedure
All the following performed from gedan barai	
Age Uke/Mae Geri/Gyaku Zuki/Gedan Barai	Forward and stepping back
Soto Ude Uke/Gyaku Zuki/Kizami Zuki/Gyaku Zuki/Gedan Barai	Forward and stepping back
Uchi Uke /Kizami Zuki/Gyaku Zuki/Gedan Barai	Forward and stepping back
Shuto Uke/ Kizami Mawashi Geri/Nukite/Shuto Uke	Forward and stepping back
All following basics will be performed starting and ending in jiyu dachi	
Kizami Zuki, Mae Geri, Oi Zuki Jodan, Gyaku zuki, Gedan Barai	Forward and stepping back
Kizami Mawashi Geri/turn Ushiro Geri/Uraken/Ghaku Zuki	Forward turn the same back
Kizami Kekomi/stepping forward Mae Geri/Uraken/Gyaku Zuki	Forward turn the same back
Gyaku Zuki, Mae Geri, Mawashi Geri, turning Shuto uchi, Gyaku Zuki	Forward turn the same back
Mae Geri/Mawashi Geri/Uraken/Gyaku Zuki/Gedan Barai	Forward turn the same back
Mae Geri/Kekomi/Shuto Uchi/Gyaku Zuki/Gedan Barai	Forward turn the same back
Ushiro Geri	Forward turn the same back
Gyaku Zuki/ Mawashi Geri Uraken/Gyaku Zuki	Forward turn the same back
Kekomi, Uraken	Forward turn the same back
Step up Ushiro Mawashi Geri	Forward turn the same back
Keage Kekomi (same leg) from kiba dachi	Forward turn the same back
Mae Geri/Kekomi/Ushiro Geri	On the spot

KUMITE

Kaeshion Ippon Kumite	-	Sets 1 & 2 (when performing these kumites they will be in groups of three)
Jiyu Ippon Kumite	-	Sets 1 & 2 (when performing these kumites they will be in groups of three)

KATA

Bassai Dai - plus any previous kata

See pages 145 - 158

SHODAN - BLACK BELT - 1ST DEGREE

KIHON

All following basics will be performed starting and ending in jiyu dachi

5	Kizami Zuki, Mae Geri, Oi Zuki Jodan, Gyaku Zuki, Gedan Barai
5	Age Uke, Mae Geri, Gyaku Zuki, Gedan Barai
5	Soto Uke, Gyaku Zuki, Kizami Zuki, Gyaku Zuki, Gedan Barai
5	Uchi Uke, Kizami Zuki, Gyaku Zuki, Gedan Barai
5	Shuto Uke, Kizami Mawshi Geri, Nukite, Shuto Uke
5	Mae Geri, Mawashi Geri, Uraken, Gyaku Zuki, Gedan Barai
5	Mae Geri, Kekomi, Shuto Uchi, Gyaku Zuki, Gedan Barai
5	Kizami Mawashi Geri, turn Ushiro Geri, Uraken, Gyaku Zuki
5	Kizami Kekomi, stepping forward Mae Geri, Uraken, Gyaku Zuki
5	Gyaku Zuki, Mae Geri, Mawashi Geri, turning Shuto Uchi, Gyaku Zuki
5	Ushiro Geri
5	Gyaku Zuki, Mawashi Geri, Uraken, Gyaku Zuki
5	Kekomi, Uraken
5	Kizami Zuki Jodan, step up Ushiro Mawashi Geri
5	Keage, Kekomi same leg (from kiba dachi)
5	Mae Geri, Kekomi, Ushiro Geri (on the spot)

KUMITE

Kihon Ippon Kumite	-	Sets 1 to 3 (when performing these kumites they will be in groups of thr
Jiyu Ippon Kumite	-	Sets 1 to 3 (when performing these kumites they will be in groups of thr
		Plus Jiyu kumite (free sparring)

KATA

Kankudai -   Ji'in, Wankan plus any previous kata

Written Exam plus Oral Exam.

NIDAN - BLACK BELT - 2ND DEGREE

All following basics will be performed starting and ending in jiyu dachi

HON

Kizami Zuki, Mae Geri, Oi Zuki Jodan, Gyaku Zuki, Gedan Barai
Age Uke, Mae Geri, Gyaku Zuki, Gedan Barai
Soto Uke, Gyaku Zuki, Kizami Zuki, Gyaku Zuki, Gedan Barai
Uchi Uke, Kizami Zuki, Gyaku Zuki, Gedan Barai
Shuto Uke, Kizami Mawshi Geri, Nukite, Shuto Uke
Mae Geri, Mawashi Geri, Uraken, Gyaku Zuki, Gedan Barai
Mae Geri, Kekomi, Shuto Uchi, Gyaku Zuki, Gedan Barai
Kizami Mawashi Geri, turn Ushiro Geri, Uraken, Gyaku Zuki
Kizami Kekomi, stepping forward Mae Geri, Uraken, Gyaku Zuki
Gyaku Zuki, Mae Geri, Mawashi Geri, turning Shuto Uchi, Gyaku Zuki
Ushiro Geri
Gyaku Zuki, Mawashi Geri, Uraken, Gyaku Zuki
Kekomi, Uraken
Kizami Zuki Jodan, step up Ushiro Mawashi Geri
Keage, Kekomi same leg (from kiba dachi)
Mae Geri, Kekomi, Ushiro Geri (on the spot)

JMITE

non Ippon Kumite	Sets 3, 4, and 5 (when performing these kumites they will be in groups of three)
yu Ippon Kumite	Sets 3, 4 and 5 (when performing these kumites they will be in groups of three)
nbon Kumite	Set 1 – 4 (both sides)
kuri Jiyu Kumite	Jodan, Chudan, Mae Geri, Kekomi, Mawashi Geri, Ushiro Geri
Kata	Suna Kake No Kom

ATA

choice of one of the following kata's with bunkai.

nkusho, Nijushiho, and Enpi

owledge of Jion and Jitte is required

s any previous kata

SANDAN - BLACK BELT - 3RD DEGREE

BASICS
Demonstrating against a stationary target on all Shotokan basic techniques.

KUMITE

Kihon Ippon Kumite	Sets 1 - 7

(when performing these kumites they will be in groups of three)

Jiyu Ippon Kumite	Sets 1 - 5

(when performing these kumites they will be in groups of three)

Plus any other previous kumites of the examiners choice

Jiyu Kumite against five consecutive Sandans – this Kumite should be performed non-stop and contir
for the duration of 10 minutes.

Kata

The students Tokui Kata with explanation of bunkai.

Bassai Sho, Chinte, Meikyo, Sochin, Tekki Sandan, Tekki Nidan, Gankaku and Hangetsu

Oral Examination

Examination of teaching ability

Sensei G. Sahota demonstrating Yoko Geri Kekomi

A club demonstration

TISKA PHOTOGRAPHS

Various photos of Sensei

TISKA PHOTOGRAPHS

Demonstrating bunkai with Mr. Barker

Filming studio with some senior grades

DUBAI 2008

Dubai 2010 Master Course

Italy 2011 - Sensei relaxing after Master Course

Sensei with England Team.

From left to right

Gary Richardson, Lee Stockley, Depace Mistry, Najinder Sehmbi, Sensei, Alistair Cullen, Conor Stephens, Dipak Matharu

*Tiska International
Championships
South Africa vs England
2009*

DUBAI 2013 TISKA PHOTOGRAPHS

TISKA PHOTOGRAPHS

TISKA PHOTOGRAPHS

Sensei with Roy Hazelwood, Chief Instructor of TSKAGB

*Left to Right: R. Reid, R. Hazelwood, G. Sahota –
Winners of the Open Championship 1979*

A presentation by Sensei Kanazawa at Slough in 1991

GLOSSARY

e (uke): *Rising (block)*
e (zuki): *Rising (punch)*
e: *Red*
: *Blue*
hi barai: *Foot sweep*
hIkubi: *Ankle*
ama: *Head*
ase: *Combined*

rai: *Parry*
ssai Dai: *To storm a fortress Kata*
: *Staff*
jutsu: *Techniques of the staff*
do: *Bu=warrior, Do=the way*
jutsu: *Bu=warrior, Jutsu=technique*
nkai: *Application taken directly from kata, matching movements exactly*

a: *Brown*
ikara: *Strength*
ikara no kyojaku: *Manner of using strength, degree of power*
oku: *Straight*
udan: *Middle level*

chi: *Stance*
n: *Level, rank, degree*
: *The way, spiritual path*
jo: *Training hall*
jo kun: *Dojo oath*
ryoku: *Effort (noun); make effort (verb)*

nbusen: *Performance line (e.g. kata)*
pi: *Elbow*
pi Uchi: *Elbow Strike*
getsu uke: *Circle foot block*
oy: *Relax*
pi: *Flying swallow (KATA)*

do (dachi): *Rooted (stance)*
mikomi geri: *Stamping kick*

nkaku: *Crane on a rock (KATA)*
iwan: *Outside of forearm (ulnar side)*

Gamae: *Ready*
Gasshuku: *Course, gathering*
Gedan: *Lower level*
Gedan barai: *Lower level parry*
Gedan zuki: *Lower level punch*
Geri: *Kick*
Gi: *Training suit / uniform*
Gohon kumite: *5-step sparring*
Goshin jutsu: *Self defence*
Gyaku (zuki): *Reverse (punch)*
Gyaku kansetsu: *Against the joint*

Hachiji (dachi): *Natural open leg (stance)*
Hai: *Yes*
Haishu: *Back of hand*
Haisoku: *Instep (literally: back of the foot)*
Haito: *Ridge hand*
Haito Uchi: *Ridge hand strike*
Haiwan: *Back of forearm*
Hajime: *Start, begin*
Hana: *Nose*
Hangetsu (dachi): *Half-moon (stance)*
Hangetsu: *Half moon (KATA)*
Hanmi (hanme): *Half-facing position; hips open*
Hanshi: *Higher teaching - after 8th Dan*
Hansoku chui: *Warned for infringement of rules (public warning)*
Hara: *Belly, lower abdomen; concept of spiritual centre*
Hasami: *Scissors*
Heian: *Peaceful mind (KATA)*
Heiko (dachi): *Parallel (stance)*
Heisoku (dachi): *Informal attention (stance)*
Hidari: *Left*
Hikite: *Pulling hand; reaction hand (position)*
Hikite gamae: *Hand pulled back position*
Hikiwake: *Draw*
Hiraken: *Foreknuckle fist*
Hitai: *Forehead*
Hiza (geri): *Knee (kick)*
Hiza: *Knee*

Hizagashira: *Knee cap*
Hoken: *Covered fist; "cover or hide the fist"*
Hombu: *Central / HQ dojo*
Hyosh: *Timing*

Iee Iie: *No*
Inyo: *Active and passive / Attack and defence*
Ippon: *Point won in a match*
Ippon ken: *One knuckle fist*
Ippon nukite: *One finger spear hand*

Jiin: *Temple grounds*
Jinchu: *Vital spot just under the nose*
Jion: *From the Temple of Jion (KATA)*
Jitte: *Temple hands / Ten hands (KATA)*
Jiyu (kumite): *Free (sparring)*
Jo: *Short stick*
Jo: *Upper*
Jodan: *Upper level*
Juji (uke): *X (block)*
Junbi-undo: *Warm ups*

Ka: *Person or practitioner*
Kage Uke: *Hooking block*
Kage (zuki): *Hook (punch)*
Kaishin: *Full arm extension*
Kaishu: *Open hand*
Kaiten: *Rotation*
Kakato: *Heel*
Kake-hiki: *Catching and pulling block*
Kakiwake: *Wedge*
Kakushi waza: *Hidden techniques*
Kakuto: *Bent wrist*
Kamae: *Posture*
Kamaete: *Action – Take up position*
Kami: *Hair*
Kanku dai / sho: *To view the sky large / small (KATA)*
Kansetsu geri: *Kick to knee joint*
Kansetsu waza: *Joint breaking techniques*
Kara: *Empty; Chinese*

GLOSSARY

Karate ni sentenashi: *There is no first attack in karate*
Kasumi: *Temple [of head]*
Kata: *Prearranged sequence of techniques*
Keage geri: *Snap (rising) kick*
Keitai no hoji: *Correct postitioning*
Keito (uke): *Chicken head wrist (block)*
Kekomi: *Thrust*
Ken: *Fist = knuckled*
Kenpo: *Old China hand*
Kentsui: *Hammer fist*
Keri waza: *Kicking techniques*
Ki: *Spirit, inner power*
Kiai: *Shout; 'Energy union', life force happening*
Kiba (dachi): *Straddle or horse (stance)*
Kihon (waza): *Basic (techniques)*
Kihon Ippon Kumite: *Basic one step sparring*
Kiiro: *Yellow*
Kime: *Focus, tension – control of power*
Kin geri: *Groin kick*
Kizami (zuki): *Jabbing (punch)*
Kobudo: *Classical martial arts of Japanese warrior weapons*
Ko-bujitsu: *Old martial arts*
Kohai-sempai: *Junior-senior*
Kokoro: *Spirit, soul, heart, mind – mental attitude*
Kokutsu (dachi): *Back (stance)*
Kokyo: *Breathing*
Kokyu chikara: *Strength applied while inhaling*
Koryu: *Classical martial traditions*
Kosa (uke): *Cross (block)*
Kosa ashi: *Cross stepping*
Kosa dachi: *Cross feet stance*
Koshi: *Ball of the foot (literally: tiger foot)*
Koto!: *At end of dojo kun means 'we make it a rule to obey the kun'*
Ku: *Emptiness*
Kubi: *Neck*
Kumi bo: *Bo fighting*
Kumite: *Sparring*

Kun: *Motto or Oath*
Kuro (obi): *Black (belt)*
Kuzushi waza: *Art of destroying opponent's balance by throwing and sweeping*
Kyu: *Rank below black belt*
Kyudo: *Way of the Bow – Japanese archery*
Kyusho: *Vital spot*
Kyusho jutsu: *Pressure points*

Ma-ai: *Distance (ing)*
Mae: *Front*
Mae Geri: *Front Kick*
Makiwara: *Striking Post*
Makiwara: *Coiled ropes or braided straw*
Makoto: *Sincerity, Truth*
Mamoru: *To keep (Chinese character meaning defend/protect)*
Manji uke: *Angular block*
Mawashi: *Round House*
Mawashi Geri: *Roundhouse kick*
Mawashi Zuki: *Roundhouse punch*
Mawate: *Turn*
Midori: *Green*
Migamae: *Physical preparation*
Migi: *Right*
Mikazuki (geri): *Cresent (kick)*
Misekake: *A feint*
Mizu No Kokoro: *IMind lik water, calmness of mind*
Mo ichi do: *One more time*
Mokuso (Mokso): *Meditation, emptying the mind*
Mokuso: *Meditation*
Morote: *Augmented*
Morote Uke: *Augmented block*
Morote Zuki: *Augmented punch*
Moto Dachi: *Reduced Zenkutsu*
Murasaki: *Purple*
Musubi (Dachi): *Informal Attention (Stance) – linked feet*

Nagashi uke: *Sweeping block*
Naihanchi: *Sideways fighting or surreptitious steps*

Naiwan: *Near side of the arm – inside of forearm (radial side)*
Nakadaka Ippon Ken: *Middle finger one knuckle fist*
Nami Ashi (Gaeshi): *Inside snapping leg block*
Nami gaeshi: *Ruturing wave*
Naore: *Return to Yoi*
Neko ashi (dachi): *Cat (stance)*
Nidan geri: *Two level kick*
Nihon nukite: *Two finger strike*
Niju kun: *Twenty precepts (Funakosh*
Nukite: *Spear hand (finger tip strike)*

Obi: *Belt*
Oi (Zuki): *Lunge (Punch)*
Oi Ashi: *Stepping*
Okinawan Te: *Okinawan School of Karate*
Omonzuru: *To respect/attack or give importance to*
Omote: *Positive; The front – techniqu of a ryu revealed to the public*
Orenji: *Orange*
Osae –Uke: *Pressing Block*
Oshi – Ateru: *X (block)*
Otoshi: *Dropping/Downward*
Oyo: *Implications of Kata where movement altered in some way*

Rei: *Bow*
Reigi: *Etiquette. Manner in Karate Do*
Ren Zuki: *Combination Punching*
Renoji Dachi: *L Stance*
Ryo: *Both*
Ryowan: *Both sides*
Ryu: *School*

Sabaki: *Motion*
Sagi ashi dachi: *Heron leg posture*
Sai: *Iron dagger protected by two lateral hooks. Sai's blade = length of forearm*
Sanbon (kumite): *3-step (Sparring)*
Sanchin dachi: *Hour glass stance*

GLOSSARY

sh Ashi: *Stepping across/ Extending the foot*

ken: *Forefist*

retsu: *Line up*

za: *Kneeling position (Meditation posture)*

npai: *Senior*

nsei: *Teacher or master.*

nshu: *Contestant*

ihan: *Master teacher 'A model for the rest'*

ihon nukite: *Four finger spear hand strike*

iko dachi: *Square stance*

ime-waza: *Strangles, chokes*

inpan: *Judge, referee*

itei (kata): *Compulsory (kata) that must be learnt*

izen: *Natural*

izentai: *Natural (stance) position*

o: *Hand, palm*

omen: *Hips square on*

oshinsha: *A beginner*

ushin: *Referee*

iro: *White*

izentai: *Natural stance*

obu: *Competition*

oto Nijukkun: *Twenty principles*

uto: *Knife hand*

uto Uchi: *Knife hand strike*

uwan: *Underside of forearm*

chin Dachi: *Diagonal straddle leg stance*

kumen: *Side*

kumen awase uke: *Side combined block*

kutei: *Sole of foot*

kuto: *Foot edge, sword foot*

to (ude uke): *Outside (forearm block)*

igetsu: *Solar plexus (water moon)*

kui uke: *Scooping block*

ne: *Shin*

ri ashi: *Shuffling (make distance by stepping up to front leg with back leg and step out with front leg - same stance)*

Tai no shinshuku: *Degree of expansion or contraction*

Taikyoku: *First cause*

Tai-sabaki: *Body evasion techniques*

Taiso: *Limbering up exercises*

Tameshi-wari: *Breaking*

Tanden: *Centre of gravity*

Tate: *Vertical*

Tate Zuki: *Vertical fist punch*

Te: *Hand*

Teiji dachi: *T stance*

Teisho: *Palm heel*

Tekubi: *Wrist*

Ten-No-Kata: *Kata of the heaven*

Tettsui: *Bottom fist (iron hammer)*

Te waza: *Hand technique*

Tobi geri: *Jumping kicks*

Tobi Tettsui Uchi: *Jumping hammer fist strike*

Tokui: *Favourite, speciality, forte*

Tsukami-uke: *Grasping block*

Tsuki: *Punching*

Tsumasaki: *Tips of (toes/fingers)*

Tsuru Ashi Dachi: *Crane Leg Stance*

Tsutsumi: *Concealed*

Tuite: *Manipulation (of joints)*

Tyakugan: *Aiming points*

Uchi: *Strike*

Uchi (Ude Uke): *Inside (Forearm block)*

Uchi-hachiji dachi: *IInverted open leg stance*

Ude: *Forearm*

Ude/Wan: *Arm*

Uke: *Block*

Uke-waza: *Techniques of receiving*

Unsoku: *Stepping techniques; Moving the feet*

Unsu:

Ura (Zuki): *Close (punch)*

Uraken: *Back fist*

Ushiro: *Reverse, back, to the rear*

Ushiro geri: *Back kick*

Uwagi: *Gi top*

Wa: *Harmony*

Wan: *Arm*

Washide: *Eagle hand*

Waza: *Techniques, skills*

Waza no kankyu: *Speed of movement*

Waza-ari: *Almost a point, half point*

Yakusoku (kumite): *Prearranged (sparring)*

Yama (zuki): *U (punch)*

Yame (yamae): *Stop*

Yashinau: *To make grow/foster/to form*

Yasumi (yasume): *Rest, at ease*

Yoi: *Ready*

Yoi no kisin: *Spirit of getting ready*

Yoko: *Side*

Yoko empi: *Side elbow*

Yoko geri: *Side kick*

Yori ashi: *Sliding / gliding movement*

Yudansha: *Black belt holders*

Za zen: *Seated meditation*

Zanshin: *State of relaxed alertness, remaining on guard. Thought; "Continuing mind"*

Zenkutsu dachi: *Front stance*

Zenwan: *Forearm*

Zuban: *Gi trousers*

Zuki: *Punch*

THE ENGLISH – JAPANESE NUMBERING TABLES 1–100

1 – ICHI

2 – NI

3 – SAN

4 – SHI

5 – GO

6 – ROKU

7 – SHICHI

8 – HACHI

9 – KU

10 – JYU

11 – JYU ICHI

12 – JYU NI

13 – JYU SAN

14 – JYU SHI

15 – JYU GO

16 – JYU ROKU

17 – JYU SHICHI

18 – JYU HACHI

19 – JYU KU

20 – NIJYU

21 – NIJYU ICHI

22 – NIJYU NI

23 – NIJYU SAN

24 – NIJYU SHI

25 – NIJYU GO

26 – NIJYU ROKU

27 – NIJYU SHICHI

28 – NIJYU HACHI

29 – NIJYU KU

30 – SANJYU

31 – SANJYU ICHI

32 – SANJYU NI

33 – SANJYU SAN

34 – SANJYU SHI

35 – SANJYU GO

36 – SANJYU ROKU

37 – SANJYU SHICHI

38 – SANJYU HACHI

39 – SANJYU KU

40 – YONJYU

41 – YONJYU ICHI

42 – YONJYU NI

43 – YONJYU SAN

44 – YONJYU SHI

45 – YONJYU GO

46 – YONJYU ROKU

47 – YONJYU SHICHI

48 – YONJYU HACHI

49 – YONJYU KU

50 – GOJYU

51 – GOJYU ICHI

52 – GOJYU NI

53 – GOJYU SAN

54 – GOJYU SHI

55 – GOJYU GO

56 – GOJYU ROKU

57 – GOJYU SHICHI

58 – GOJYU HACHI

59 – GOJYU KU

60 – ROKUJYU

61 – ROKUJYU ICHI

62 – ROKUJYU NI

63 – ROKUJYU SAN

64 – ROKUJYU SHI

65 – ROKUJYU GO

66 – ROKUJYU ROKU

67 – ROKUJYU SHICHI

68 – ROKUJYU HACHI

69 – ROKUJYU KU

70 – SHICHIJYU

71 – SHICHIJYU ICHI

72 – SHICHIJYU NI

73 – SHICHIJYU SAN

74 – SHICHIJYU SHI

75 – SHICHIJYU GO

76 – SHICHIJYU ROKU

77 – SHICHIJYU SHICHI

78 – SHICHIJYU HACHI

79 – SHICHIJYU KU

80 – HACHIJYU

81 – HACHIJYU ICHI

82 – HACHIJYU NI

83 – HACHIJYU SAN

84 – HACHIJYU SHI

85 – HACHIJYU GO

86 – HACHIJYU ROKU

87 – HACHIJYU SHICHI

88 – HACHIJYU HACHI

89 – HACHIJYU KU

90 – KYUJYU

91 – KYUJYU ICHI

92 – KYUJYU NI

93 – KYUJYU SAN

94 – KYUJYU SHI

95 – KYUJYU GO

96 – KYUJYU ROKU

97 – KYUJYU SHICHI

98 – KYUJYU HACHI

99 – KYUJYU KU

100 – HYAKU

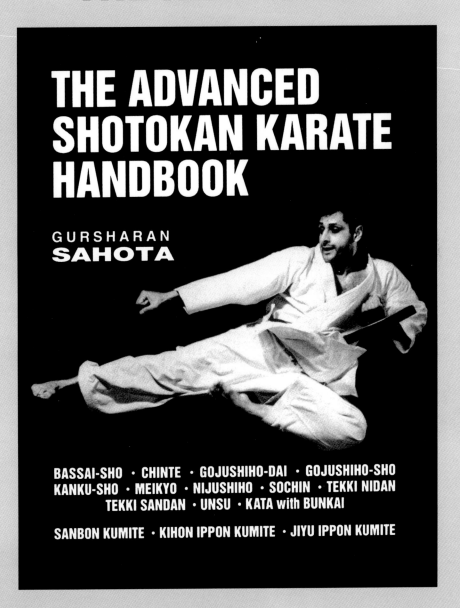

DOJO KUN

THE DOJO KARATEKA OATH
"Dojo Kun"

•

"Hitotsu! Jinkaku Kansei ni Tsutomuru Koto"
(One! To Strive For The Perfection of Character!)

•

"Hitotsu! Makoto No Michi O Mamoru Koto!"
(One! To Defend The Paths Of Truth!)

•

"Hitotsu! Doryoku No Seishin O Yashinau Koto!"
(One! To Foster The Spirit Of Effort!)

•

"Hitotsu! Reigi O Omonzuru Koto!"
(One! To Honour The Principles of Etiquette!)

•

"Hitotsu! Kekki No Yu O Imashimuru Koto!"
(One To Guard Against Impetuous Courage!)